The United States Trade Deficit of the 1980s

The United States Trade Deficit of the 1980s

ORIGINS, MEANINGS, AND POLICY RESPONSES

Chris C. Carvounis

Q

QUORUM BOOKS
NEW YORK
WESTPORT, CONNECTICUT
LONDON

Library of Congress Cataloging-in-Publication Data

Carvounis, Chris C.
  The United States trade deficit of the 1980s.

  Bibliography: p.
  Includes index.
  1. Balance of trade—United States.
2. United States—Commerce.   I. Title.
II. Title: Trade deficit of the 1980s.
HF3031.C37   1987   382.1'7'0973   87-2561
ISBN 0-89930-219X (lib. bdg. : alk. paper)

Library of Congress Catalog Card Number: 87-2561
ISBN: 0-89930-219-X

First published in 1987 by Quorum Books

Greenwood Press, Inc.
88 Post Road West, Westport, Connecticut 06881

Printed in the United States of America

The paper used in this book complies with the
Permanent Paper Standard issued by the National
Information Standards Organization (Z39.48-1984).

10 9 8 7 6 5 4 3 2 1

CONTENTS

TABLES

INTRODUCTION

APPROACH TO THE TOPIC

By 1985 the U.S. trade deficit had become a problem in its own right. Following decades at near-balance, America's merchandise trade account turned sharply negative in 1981 and 1982. This weakening in our trade performance, however, could be readily explained as an effect of the second oil shock which had raised our own energy-import bill and dampened demand in our main export markets. Moreover, the United States enjoyed a large and growing surplus in its international capital account, with American investments abroad far surpassing foreign investments here, and net earnings on these assets helping to offset the trade imbalance. The gap between imports and exports widened greatly in 1983 and 1984, eating away at our capital surplus, but this too could be conveniently dispelled. The aftermath of the oil shock continued to plague the economies of our major trading partners, and, better still, America had successfully recovered from the oil trauma as domestic growth resumed at a brisk pace. This expansion, we were told, had unleashed a surge of pent-up import demand at home and earnings on these sales would soon enable other countries to increase their consumption of American goods and services. But in 1985 internal growth slowed, exports remained flat, imports continued to climb, and America shouldered a heavy burden of trade-related external debt. It was no longer possible to dismiss the trade deficit as a symptom of some other ailment or a temporary aberration: it had become a distinct, chronic, and potentially debilitating malady in and of itself.

Acknowledged as such, the trade imbalance became a central issue in American politics, as the search for a means to "fix" it began. A national debate emerged pitting protectionists against advocates of free and open trade. To be sure, American producers hard hit by import competition had been clamoring for relief for some time, and their complaints had been selectively addressed by the government through a string of import-restraining policy measures. But in 1985 the protectionist push coalesced and intensified, with a severely pressured Congress calling on President Reagan to adopt an aggressive campaign against the unfair practices of our foreign rivals and hastily preparing its own "get tough" legislation should he fail to do so. The president responded by reiterating America's long-standing commitment to free trade, negotiating a series of bilateral and multilateral agreements to limit the flow of foreign goods into the economy, and appropriating the "fair trade" rhetoric of the opposition, all in a concerted effort to head off even sterner action by the legislature. As individual positions shifted and party lines were crossed the American public was left at a loss to discern just what their nation's trade policy was beyond being woefully ineffective. In a poll conducted in mid-1986, it was reported that 70 percent of those surveyed were not sure if the Democratic Party was, "generally speaking," for free trade or for import limitations, while 56 percent were uncertain about the stand of the Republican Party.[1]

In large part, America's ongoing trade debate remains muddy because its organization along protectionist/free market lines does more to obscure the overall nature of the problem at hand than it does to articulate it. Fixated with remedies, the current arguments fail to take adequate account of the causes and consequences of the trade imbalance. In this sense, it is as if two physicians were prescribing alternative cures without performing either a diagnosis or prognosis for the patient. The present study aims to remedy this deficiency by using a two-track analysis of the trade deficit, presenting two comprehensive and contrasting versions of its origins (Chapter 2), its meanings (Chapter 3), and its indicated policy responses (Chapter 4) alongside each other. This framework will enable the reader to assess the relative merits of each viewpoint and to gain a composite picture of the trade problem as a whole far superior to that which either perspective can provide alone.

What I will be referring to as the monetarist interpretation of the trade deficit locates its origins in an excess of domestic demand. It pivots on the straightforward premise that when a nation consumes more in value than it produces, a negative external balance results. The American trade deficit is rooted in cyclical, macroeconomic factors of comparatively recent vintage, principally a federal government budget deficit not matched by sufficient internal savings. The government's fiscal profligacy has contributed to the deterioration of our trade account through two interrelated mechanisms. First, by overstimulating the American economy, it has led to immoderately high import demand at the same time as the governments of our chief trading partners have curbed import consumption by adhering to far less expansionary policies. Second, in order to finance the budget deficit, the federal government has vastly enlarged its use of credit, causing real interest rates in the United States to stay well above those available in the economies of our competitors. This, in turn, has attracted an inflow of capital from abroad as foreign investors have converted their own savings into U.S. currency to take advantage of higher yields, thereby bidding up the value of the dollar and eroding the price competitiveness of dollar-denominated goods in global markets.

From the monetarist standpoint, the central meaning of the trade deficit resides in its impact upon growth in the United States. Quite obviously, when consumers forego purchases of American-made wares in favor of products made elsewhere, this reduces current and potential output in the United States. As importantly, accumulated external debt stemming from an excess of import consumption must be serviced. Thus, resources must be transferred abroad which would otherwise be used to finance productive investment at home.

The monetarist antidote centers on removing impediments to the natural workings of market forces. It calls for bringing public expenditures into line with revenues, allowing the Federal Reserve Board to restrict the growth of monetary aggregates without evoking a rise in domestic interest rates. As an ancillary action, the United States may exhort slow-growth nations enjoying bilateral surpluses with it to reflate their economies through less austere fiscal and monetary policies, but we cannot fault them should they resist this course since, at bottom, they will be guilty merely of macroeconomic prudence.

The structuralist understanding of the trade deficit's causes points to prolonged, secular, microeconomic trends that have gradually undermined America's capacity to produce more output from a given level of input, i.e., to a broad decline in productivity growth relative to that of our trade competitors. The erosion of our formerly secure advantages in real factors of production—capital, labor, and applied technology—is the source of our diminished ability to compete. In addition, several of our rivals have adopted highly effective means for mobilizing their productive resources in the form of government-orchestrated industrial policies and outward-looking corporate strategies, leaving us way behind on both counts.

As the structuralists see it, the ultimate meaning of the trade deficit is nothing less than the wholesale deindustrialization of the United States. With foreign producers capturing larger shares of global markets in basic industries, our factories will eventually shut down, many being dismantled by American multinational corporations seeking to regain factor advantages by moving production offshore. This will necessarily entail a reduction in American living standards as our workers will be crowded out of high-productivity, high-pay manufacturing jobs into low-productivity, low-wage service employment.

According to the structuralists, what America requires, and our successful trade adversaries have already accomplished, is the implementation of a globally competitive industrial policy. This need can be partially fulfilled simply through a closer coordination of existing policies that impact upon the international competitiveness of our industries. More significantly, the structuralists argue that the United States must erect a publicly managed institutional apparatus for channeling national resources into

industries that possess a competitive edge and easing the adjustment of those unable to meet the foreign challenge.

MAGNITUDE OF THE PROBLEM

Since the early 1970s, the importance of international commerce to the American economy has swelled enormously. Between 1970 and 1982, trade as a proportion of the country's Gross
National Product rose by 140 percent, compared to respective
increases of 44 percent, 36 percent, and 80 percent for Japan,
West Germany, and France.[2] By 1985, exports accounted for
some 20 percent of the nation's manufactured output,[3] while
roughly 40 percent of its agricultural products were sold overseas.[4] On the other side of the ledger, imports command about
one-fourth of the American market for manufactured goods and
some 70 percent of all U.S. industries are exposed to foreign
competition.[5] These figures actually understate the weight of foreign trade since they do not reflect its influence upon domestically oriented economic activity dependent upon export and import-competing industries.

Before turning to an examination of U.S. trade data for the
1980s, a brief word about these figures is in order. The reader
may have encounterd trade statistics seemingly at odds with each
other—with, for instance, the American merchandise trade deficit for 1984 being alternatively stated as $123.3 billion, $107.9
billion, $108.3 billion, and $101.5 billion.[6] These disparities are
due to the fact that several government agencies issue official
trade data, each using a different method of computation. Moreover, foreign governments and international organizations em-
ploy their own unique systems for calculating cross-border
transactions. In what follows, I will rely upon statistics prepared
through the U.S. Department of Commerce's methods, that is,
c.i.f. imports (cost, insurance, freight) and f.a.s. exports (free
alongside), which reflect the landed cost of goods including
transport and insurance.

After decades in which the United States posted extremely
modest deficits and surpluses on its merchandise trade account,

a large shortfall was recorded in 1981 ($27.3 billion), followed by
an even greater deficit ($31.8 billion) in 1982. In 1983, our ex-
ports reached the $200 billion mark, but were outpaced by im-
ports by a margin of $57.6 billion. The decline of America's trade
performance accelerated in 1984, exports rising less than $20 bil-
lion as imports mushroomed nearly $90 billion, leaving a whop-
ping $123.3 billion negative imbalance. This record was eclipsed
in 1985 as exports actually fell some $4 billion and imports grew
another $25 billion, resulting in a $148.5 billion deficit for the
year. The first half of 1986 witnessed a continuation of this trend.
In fact, the January–June trade deficit amounted to $83.9 billion,
compared to $69.3 billion in the first six months of 1985,[7] and
the *monthly* deficit for July 1986 reached a record $18.7 billion,
with imports being twice as large as exports for the first time in
recorded history.[8] Preliminary estimates of the trade imbalance
for 1986 as a whole project a deficit of between $170 billion and
$200 billion. At the lower figure, the *rate* of increase in the trade
deficit is beginning to subside; at the higher one, it is gaining
momentum.

In essence, what has occurred over the 1980s is that American
deliveries abroad have remained virtually unchanged, while foreign shipments to the United States have expanded at an as-
tounding tempo, rising in volume terms by over 65 percent between 1980 and mid-1985.[9] From 1979 through the first quarter
of 1986, real American nonagricultural exports declined fraction-
ally as a percentage of real domestic sales, but nonoil imports
more than doubled.[10] What this suggests is that the core of the
trade deficit problem does indeed lie within the United States
itself in the form of skyrocketing purchases of foreign goods.
True, the imbalance would have been mitigated had American
exports grown at a reasonable clip, but it is import growth that
has been the phenomenal departure from what might have been
expected.

Table 1 illustrates the inordinately rapid growth of imports to
the United States. It displays import-penetration ratios for both
capital goods and consumer goods, these ratios being constructed by dividing imports of goods in each sector by total
American expenditures in each, *excluding* automotive and food
products. What we find, in general, is that foreign capital and

consumer goods have increased their market share in the United States at a very fast pace over the term, with capital goods (items employed in production processes) rising more swiftly than consumer products. Without advancing too far ahead, the correlation of these ratios with real GNP growth in the United States and the real exchange value of the dollar is at the heart of the monetarist understanding of the deficit. For both sectors, import market shares spread most rapidly when real American economic growth rebounded in mid-1983 and the dollar began its prolonged upward spiral to the first quarter of 1985. At the same time, however, and especially in the case of consumer goods, the slowing of output growth in the United States and the fall of the dollar since the onset of 1985 has *not* led to a sustained decline in the import penetration of the American economy, casting doubt on the explanatory power of the growth/exchange rate explication of the trade deficit. Since we shall cover the monetarist rendition of the causes of the trade imbalance in Chapter 2 (with further reference to this table), at this juncture we need merely note that an increasing share of the products we consume *and* an even larger share of the means by which we produce goods are imported from abroad, and that both have periodically resisted changes in macroeconomic conditions.

BILATERAL TRADE BALANCES

Although the total U.S. trade balances is the sum of America's bilateral trade balances with the 130-odd nations with whom we have commercial relations, the reader must be cautioned that thinking of the overall balance as simply the arithmetical aggregation of zero-sum, two-party trade handicaps our understanding of it on at least two fronts. First, in practice, trade relations between countries must be seen in a multilateral context as integral parts of the global trading system. "In a well-functioning multilateral trading system," Rachel McCulloch observes, "there is no reason to expect any two nations to have balanced trade even in the long-run."[11] Indeed, when we look, for example, at the trade conflicts that have erupted between the United States and the European Economic Community, the majority of these

Table 1
Penetration Ratios for U.S. Imports of Capital Goods and Consumer Goods Correlated with Real U.S. GNP Growth and the Real Exchange Value of the Dollar, 1980–1985

Year & Quarter	Growth Rate of Real GNP (in percent)	Real Exchange Value of the Dollar (1980=100)	Penetration Ratios Capital Goods	Consumer Goods
1980: Quarter 1	1.6	100.0	13.7	6.9
Quarter 2	-0.7	101.2	14.5	7.1
Quarter 3	-1.5	98.4	14.8	6.6
Quarter 4	-0.1	103.0	15.3	6.8
1981: Quarter 1	0.9	109.5	15.9	7.1
Quarter 2	3.8	119.1	16.3	7.2
Quarter 3	3.3	128.2	17.4	7.4
Quarter 4	0.6	121.9	18.3	8.0
1982: Quarter 1	-2.8	125.8	19.3	7.8
Quarter 2	-2.2	129.7	20.6	7.5
Quarter 3	-3.4	136.8	20.2	7.9
Quarter 4	-1.9	137.6	18.7	7.5
1983: Quarter 1	0.6	132.8	21.1	8.0
Quarter 2	2.5	136.6	21.9	8.4
Quarter 3	4.4	142.8	28.9	8.9
Quarter 4	6.3	143.8	26.5	9.5

1984: Quarter 1	8.1	145.0	28.2	9.9
Quarter 2	7.2	146.2	29.1	10.7
Quarter 3	6.6	156.7	30.9	11.0
Quarter 4	4.7	162.1	30.3	11.0
1985: Quarter 1	2.9	171.1	29.7	10.3
Quarter 2	1.9	162.7	27.4	10.4
Quarter 3	2.1	152.5	29.9	11.2
Quarter 4	2.5	140.6	30.1	11.3

Source: Robert A. Johnson, "U.S. International Transactions in 1985," Federal Reserve Bulletin, Vol. lxxii, No. 5 (May 1986), p. 291.

9

revolve around competition between American and Western European exports in third-country markets. Second, trade competitors are, virtually by definition, also trade partners. For instance, as Japanese exports began to lag in the first half of 1986 (largely as the consequence of a rapidly appreciating yen), this was interpreted as a wholly positive phenomenon from the standpoint of the United States. Such was, and is, not the case. For an export-led economy such as Japan's to undergo a downturn in its trade earnings also means that its capacity to increase imports of American goods and services has been pared.

With these provisos in mind, Table 2 provides a summary of American bilateral trade balances with fifteen major trading partners over the period 1983–1985, with 1981 included as a basis for comparison. In the case of the first five nations listed (Japan, Canada, Taiwan, West Germany, and Hong Kong), we discover a highly uniform pattern of unrelenting growth in our bilateral deficits, with a very strong downturn being evident in 1984. As to the next six countries (Mexico, Italy, Brazil, South Korea, the United Kingdom, and France), more of the same is apparent, with our 1981 trade surpluses against Italy and France being transformed into deficits and the modest narrowing of our trade gap with Mexico (1984) and Brazil (1985) being the product of a temporary loosening in debt-related, import-restraining austerity programs by their governments. In 1985, the largest bilateral surplus enjoyed by the United States was with the Dutch economy, followed closely by Saudi Arabia, Australia, and, ironically, the Soviet Union. The shift to a positive balance with the Saudis in 1983 was, of course, an outcome of energy conservation measures adopted in the United States, but, as previously suggested, the reduction of their oil-export earnings has led the Saudis to curb imports from the United States. With marginal exceptions, then, to say that the United States has experienced an across-the-board worsening in our bilateral trade balances is by no means an exaggeration: We must search far and wide for "bright spots" when we look at these figures.

Whenever the current U.S. trade deficit is mentioned, reference to Japan is sure to be close behind. Approximately one-third of America's entire merchandise trade gap and about one-half of its manufacturing trade deficit are embodied in two-way commerce with the Japanese. Underscoring the salience of U.S.–Japanese relations within the American trade quandary is the fact that since the early 1950s, the dramatic rise in Japan's shares of both world output and global exports has unmistakably paralleled the shrinkage of America's shares.[12] While Japan's superior export performance in third-country markets certainly contributes to these ongoing trends, the driving force is the burgeoning wave of Japanese exports to the United States. In 1981, some 24 percent of all Japanese exports were bound for the United States; by 1985, 37 percent of Japanese trade shipments were destined for America.[13]

There are at least three reasons to believe that the U.S.–Japanese trade balance will become an even more prominent part of our overall trade situation in the near term. First, while the much heralded rise of the yen against the dollar may ultimately lead to a narrowing of the trade gap between the two countries, initial 1986 trade figures show it widening further. In the first quarter of 1986, the United States ran a $15.3 billion bilateral deficit with Japan, 38 percent higher than in the first three months of 1985,[14] and although American exports to Japan increased marginally in the second quarter of 1986, they were outstripped by growing imports of Japanese goods.[15] Consequently, our trade imbalance with Japan will almost certainly become more lopsided in 1986 as a whole and possibly in 1987 as well. Second, despite the claim that recent trade negotiations to open Japanese markets to American imports and curtail "dumping" of Japanese products in the United States will serve to partially redress the disequilibrium, a genuinely comprehensive program of bilateral trade liberalization would probably have a negative impact from the American standpoint. In several critical industries, steel and automobiles for example, the U.S. government has already reached orderly marketing agreements (OMAs) with the Japanese. These "voluntary restraints" function as informal quotas on Japanese exports to America. If these self-imposed limits were dropped as part of a thoroughgoing trade liberalization program, the resulting flood of Japanese shipments to the United States would more than cancel out gains from increased American exports to Japan.[16] Finally, the fastest growing component of Japanese exports worldwide is in the high-tech sector in which the

Table 2
U.S. Bilateral Trade Balances with Fifteen Major Trading Partners, 1981, 1983–1985 (in dollars billion)

Country	1981	1983	1984	1985
Japan				
Imports from	37.7	41.2	60.4	72.4
Exports to	21.8	21.9	23.6	22.6
Balances with	-15.8	-19.3	-36.8	-49.7
Canada				
Imports from	45.9	52.1	66.9	69.4
Exports to	39.6	38.2	46.5	47.3
Balances with	-6.3	-13.9	-20.4	-22.2
Taiwan				
Imports from	8.1	11.2	16.1	17.8
Exports to	4.3	4.7	5.0	4.7
Balanceswith	-3.8	-6.5	-11.1	-13.1
West Germany				
Imports from	11.4	12.7	17.8	21.2
Exports to	10.3	8.7	9.1	9.0
Balances with	-1.1	-4.0	-8.7	-12.2
Hong Kong				
Imports from	5.4	6.4	8.9	9.0
Exports to	2.6	2.6	3.1	2.8
Balances with	-2.8	-3.8	-5.8	-6.2
Mexico				
Imports from	13.8	16.8	18.3	19.4
Exports to	17.8	9.1	12.0	13.6
Balances with	4.0	-6.5	-6.3	-5.8
Italy				
Imports from	5.2	5.5	8.5	10.4
Exports to	5.4	3.9	4.4	4.6
Balances with	0.2	-1.5	-4.1	-5.8
Brazil				
Imports from	4.5	4.9	8.3	8.1
Exports to	3.8	2.6	2.6	3.1
Balances with	-0.7	-2.4	-5.6	-5.0

	1981	1983	1984	1985
South Korea				
Imports from	5.2	7.1	10.0	10.7
Exports to	5.1	5.9	6.0	6.0
Balances with	0.1	-1.2	-4.0	-4.8
United Kingdom				
Imports from	12.8	12.5	15.0	15.6
Exports to	12.4	10.6	12.2	11.3
Balances with	-0.4	-1.8	-2.8	-3.9
France				
Import from	5.9	6.0	8.5	10.0
Exports to	7.3	6.0	6.0	6.1
Balances with	1.5	0.0	-2.5	-3.9
Netherlands				
Imports from	2.4	3.0	4.3	5.3
Exports to	8.6	7.8	7.6	7.4
Balances with	6.2	4.8	3.2	2.9
Saudi Arabia				
Imports from	14.4	3.6	4.0	2.1
Exports to	7.3	7.9	5.6	4.5
Balances with	-7.1	4.3	1.6	2.4
Australia				
Imports from	2.5	2.2	2.9	2.8
Exports to	5.2	4.8	1.0	5.4
Balances with	2.8	2.6	1.9	2.5
Soviet Union				
Imports from	0.3	0.3	0.6	0.4
Exports to	2.4	2.0	3.3	2.4
Balances with	2.1	1.7	2.7	2.0

Source: Compiled from various issues of Business America
(Department of Commerce)
Note: Due to rounding, balances given may not be
arithmetical sums.

United States previously enjoyed unchallenged dominance.[17] Thus, competition in our trade with the Japanese is likely to intensify as they increase their trade activity in this field.

Notwithstanding the fact that our largest bilateral trade deficit is with Japan, in terms of total goods exchanged, America's cardinal trading partner remains Canada, with about $120 billion in merchandise flowing across our northern border each year. American exports to Canada are more than twice as large as deliveries to Japan, being roughly equivalent with our exports to the European Economic Community.[18] Trade between the two North American allies is even more important to the Canadians. The United States receives 70 percent of all Canadian exports, and, since mid-1984, Canada's bilateral surplus with the United States has counterbalanced its trade deficits with every other region of the world. The "quiet deficit" with Canada may have been largely overshadowed by other American bilateral trade imbalances, but over the period 1980 to 1985, it has enlarged at a faster pace than its U.S.–Japanese counterpart.[19]

America's trade relations with Western Europe are complicated by the confederation of the region's industrial powers as the European Economic Community, which, above all, is a trade or customs union. Taken individually or collectively, it is with the economies of Western Europe that the United States has suffered its most acute trade reversal. In 1980, the United States boasted a $20 billion trade surplus with the region. Five years later, Western Europe registered a $21 billion surplus against the United States.[20]

In sharp contrast to America's trade relations with Japan and Canada, mutual efforts to correct the U.S.–E.E.C. trade imbalance are inhibited by the fact that Europe relies on the American market for a comparatively small share of its export sales (approximately 15 percent), the fact that its importance as an outlet for American goods has declined progressively since the mid-1970s, and the fact that the most serious trade conflicts between the two concern their respective agricultural support systems for exports to the developing world. Nevertheless, while U.S. bilateral trade relations with Western Europe are adumbrated by their competition in third-country markets, since 1980 West Germany, Italy, the United Kingdom, and France have all transformed deficits or tiny surpluses with the United States into substantial net gains. This pattern is most pronounced in the case of West Germany, whose trade surplus with the United States increased more than tenfold between 1981 and 1985. In 1985, Germany posted a $17 billion current account surplus, the world's largest after Japan, two-thirds of this excess being derived from its dealings with the United States.[21] Similar to Japan, Germany's bilateral surplus has mounted in the first half of 1986, as its exports to America have been running at a $25 billion annualized pace, but in the German case, imports of American-made goods have actually declined from 1985 levels.[22]

Once termed the "four tigers," the Newly Industrialized Countries (NICs) of East Asia, South Korea, Taiwan, Hong Kong, and Singapore were previously seen as the next import threat to the United States. The good news is that Hong Kong's exports to America have languished of late, while Singapore's export sector never really got off the ground. The bad news is that both South Korea and Taiwan, by rigorously duplicating Japan's "export or die" approach to economic development, have more than taken up the slack. Between 1981 and 1985, South Korean exports to the United States doubled, with America currently accepting some two-fifths of total Korean exports.[23] On the other hand, South Korean imports of American wares have barely budged in value, declining from 26 percent of total Korean foreign purchases in 1975 to 22 percent in 1985.[24] Following a brief respite in 1985, Korean exports to the United States increased nearly 20 percent during the first half of 1986,[25] much of this spurt coming from the first offering of Hyundai automobiles to the American buying public.

Although textiles and shoes still comprise one-half of South Korean deliveries to the United States, true to the Japanese prototype, the Koreans have progressively shifted into industries of former or current American comparative advantage. Aside from cars, South Korea is now sending us an increasing proportion of high-tech items as part of its export bundle. For example, Korean sales of semiconductors in the United States rose from $650 million in 1982 to an anticipated $1.5 billion in 1986, with a further increase to $3 billion projected for 1990.[26] Unlike Japan, and to the frustration of the United States, opportunities for

America to compensate for this growing inflow of Korean goods
through enlarged exports are inherently constrained by the small
size of Korea's domestic market.[27]

Much of what has been said about South Korea's bilateral trade
balance with the United States can be applied with equal force
to America's commercial ties with Taiwan. In 1985, Taiwan's
$13 billion surplus with America was 50 percent larger than Ja-
pan's on a per capita basis.[28] Along with South Korea, Taiwan
is classified as a developing country by the United States and is
the largest beneficiary of America's General System of Preferences (GSP) which favors exports from developing economies.
Consequently, it is not surprising that a full 40 percent of all
Taiwanese export shipments arrive at American ports of entry.[29]
Analogous to South Korea's experience, thus far 1986 has been
a banner year for the Taiwanese as they have watched their exports to the United States grow by 10 percent over the corresponding period in 1985.[30] Shared circumstances make Taiwan
and South Korea fierce competitors for lucrative niches in the
world's markets, the only major difference between the two being
Taiwan's avoidance of a large stock of external debt in contrast
to South Korea's $50 billion in outstanding foreign liabilities.

America's trade relations with Latin America are clouded by
the central datum of that continent's economic life, the existence of some $350 billion to $400 billion in unpaid external debt
(Brazil, Mexico, and Argentina accounting for over two-thirds
of that sum), a substantial portion of which is owed to American-based banks. The need to service this mountain of foreign
debt has skewed Latin American trade relations with the United
States in two ways. Under the strictures of balance-of-payments
adjustment programs, either self-imposed or mandated by their
creditors through the International Monetary Fund, Latin America's debtor economies have eliminated the flow of all but the
most essential imports from the United States since the early
1980s. Although there has been modest, if sporadic, growth in
American exports to Latin America in 1984, 1985, and the first
half of 1986, as Brazilian President Jose Sarney stated in a recent visit to Washington: "We would buy much more if we could
get some relief from our debt-servicing costs."[31] As part of the
same adjustment process, these nations have been virtually

compelled to marshal concerted export drives targeted toward the United States in order to reap the foreign exchange earnings they require to service their dollar-denominated foreign debt. Outstanding loans, then, have distorted U.S.–Latin American trade patterns, but as long as their staggering debt-service burden remains, Latin economies have no choice but to constrict imports from, and boost exports to, the United States.

SECTORAL BALANCES

Another way of parsing the total U.S. trade balance is by breaking it down into its component sectors. Up to this point, I have been speaking specifically of the merchandise trade account. This aggregation does *not* include trade in so-called "invisibles," that is, services and earnings on foreign investments, which can be combined with merchandise trade as parts of the current account balance. In itself, the merchandise trade account consists of three major sectors: manufacturing, agriculture, and petroleum products. Of these, it is America's manufacturing sector that has experienced the most drastic downturn in its balance of imports and exports. In 1980, the United States sold $13.7 billion more in manufactured wares than it purchased from abroad. In 1985, foreign producers sent $112.8 billion more in manufactures to America than they received from us, a swing of $126.5 billion in five years.[32] On the whole, America's manufactured goods have been faring far worse in global markets than any other sector of our trade. In 1985, for instance, virtually all of the deterioration in the overall U.S. trade balance was due to the weak performance of this sector.

Within manufactures, broad divisions in the trade balances of specific industry groups are apparent. Over the past twenty years, "the U.S. comparative advantage in unskilled-labor and capital-intensive products has been declining secularly . . . but the U.S. comparative advantage in high-tech products has strengthened."[33] As a rule of thumb, America's high-tech goods, e.g. computers, aircraft, pharmaceuticals, etc., *have* retained a competitive edge in international markets, but our capital-intensive,

such as steel, and low-skill, such as wearing apparel, industries
have declined from world-class to second-rate status.[34]

This broad generalization, however, requires a substantial
amount of qualification. First and foremost, our comparative advantage in technology-intensive industries has tapered since the
late 1970s as both industrialized and developing country rivals
have closed their technology gap with the United States. At a
time when the nation's trade deficit in other manufactured products rose from $15 billion to $35 billion, the U.S. trade surplus
in high-technology trade grew from $12 billion in 1972 to $40
billion in 1979.[35] But by 1985, the American high-tech surplus
had shriveled to a mere $3.6 billion.[36] Second, within specific
high-tech industries, the United States has turned in strong advances in particular product lines such as assembled computers,
while losing ground in others, such as semiconductors.[37] Finally,
at the opposite end of the spectrum, a study conducted by the
National Academy of Engineering between 1982 and 1985 concluded that under the stress of low-cost foreign competition, the
American automobile, textile, and steel industries "are expected
to experience a permanent decline from earlier levels of output,
irrespective of public policy."[38]

In the cases of steel and textiles, the Academy's summary
judgment appears to be accurate. As to automobiles, their assessment may be mistaken or, at least, premature. Granted, in
1985 the lion's share of the 6 percent growth of American imports in volume terms was due to increased purchases of Japanese and West European automobiles,[39] and by mid-1986, foreign car manufacturers held more than one-quarter of the
American automotive market.[40] But Detroit displayed surprising
resilience in 1986, launching an extraordinarily aggressive wave
of low-cost financing programs which have reportedly boosted
their sales volumes and allowed them to recapture some of the
market formerly relinquished to imports. Consequently, the distinction between globally competitive high-tech goods and sorely outgunned low-tech products is not a cut-and-dried matter:
even within industries all but written off, nimble turnabouts may
occur.

Reaching a peak surplus of $24.7 billion in 1981, the U.S. agricultural trade surplus dwindled steadily to under $8 billion in

1985,[41] with the price of American farm exports dropping 10 percent and the volume of shipments falling by 15 percent in that
year alone. The worst, however, was yet to come. In May 1986
the United States imported more agricultural goods than it exported for the first month since 1971, and successive deficits in
June and July indicate that 1986 may be the first year since the
1950s that the United States will suffer a shortfall in this sector.[42] At mid-1986, imports still account for a comparatively small
fraction of America's $400 billion a year domestic food market.
Nonetheless, at 6 percent of total sales ($24 billion), their share
has nearly doubled since 1980. In some segments, imports account for a far larger portion of domestic consumption, amounting to one-fifth of the fresh fruit and vegetable market, with
Mexican exporters alone supplying over one-half of America's
winter vegetables.

In sharp relief to the pattern for manufactures, the decline of
the U.S. agricultural trade balance is due primarily to a contraction in our sales abroad. This is most evident in the case of grains.
Between June 1985 and June 1986, American grain producers
saw their slice of global markets shrink from 36 percent to 30
percent.[43] Wheat exports in the first six months of 1986 were
some 16 percent below their level in the corresponding period of
1985, while corn exports nosedived 62 percent on the same basis.[44] The reasons behind the shocking downturn in our agricultural sector are manifold. In the main, however, American farmers have been caught in a scissors mechanism. On one flank,
advances in agricultural technology and plant genetics have resulted in a general shrinkage of world agrarian trade as major
food-importing countries have become increasingly able to meet
the bulk of their needs from internal sources. On the other, competition between food exporting countries has intensified as many
governments have enlarged farm subsidy programs to retain their
portions of a diminished pie.

Petroleum is the sole sector in which the United States has
seen some improvement in its trade balance during the 1980s.
Rapid domestic growth caused the nation's oil deficit to increase
by $4 billion in 1984 to some $55 billion. As growth began to
flag, however, 1985's petroleum deficit ebbed by some $7.5 bil-
lion. More importantly, the collapse of world oil prices from mid-

1985 to mid-1986 will undoubtedly lead to a further reduction in our net petroleum bill. For example, in the month of June 1985, with crude oil averaging $28.07 a barrel, the United States posted a deficit of $5 billion in petroleum. In the month of June 1986, however, as a barrel of crude slumped to $14.03 on average, the oil deficit came in at $3.3 billion.[45] Both oil prices and oil demand are notoriously volatile. A combination of increased consumption through prospectively faster domestic growth, decreased American production of oil and/or a reassertion of the Organization of Petroleum Exporting Countries's (OPEC) control over world petroleum flows could lead to an abrupt reversal in this positive trend. Whatever transpires, there are presently some dark clouds in the silver lining. The fall of world oil prices has had an even more positive effect upon the economies of several of our trade adversaries, e.g. Japan, South Korea, and Taiwan, and will enable them to cut production costs in their export and import-competing industries. At the same time, the United States relies upon oil-exporting countries as trade outlets for a far larger percentage of its sales than do this same set of trade rivals.[46]

Although they are not incorporated into merchandise trade account figures, international exchanges of services (insurance, banking, transport, construction, etc.) and net investment earnings comprise an extremely significant element in America's foreign trade. The chief reason for this separation is that as "invisibles," cross-border movements of services, unlike merchandise transactions, cannot be effectively monitored. Furthermore, what appears to be a larger flow of unregistered "capital flight" money into the United States has created an enormous statistical discrepancy in our current account balance, ruling out the simple extrapolation of service trade data. Hence, analysis of international service transactions is greatly hampered by the absence of completely reliable figures. According to one set of calculations reported in the *New York Times*, during 1985 the United States exported $144 billion in services (including return investment flows) and imported $122.3 billion (including remittances to foreign investors), leaving it with a surplus of around $21.7 billion for the year.[47] This, however, represents a marked decline from an estimated $41 billion service surplus for 1981.

In the subsector of net earnings on foreign investments, the inflow of foreign capital that has permitted the United States to run its huge merchandise trade deficits has led to an enlarged "paper" outflow of interest earnings. For example, in 1985, foreign holders of U.S. Treasury securities were credited with approximately $23 billion in interest payments on them, up $2 billion from the previous year. Concurrently, earnings of American banks on overseas loans decreased by about $10 billion in 1985 compared with 1984 as a consequence of loan rescheduling exercises, payment interruptions, and the sharp reduction of foreign lending since the onset of the Third World debt crisis in mid-1982.

Moreover, the United States now confronts serious challenges in services as our chief trade rivals diversify into these areas. Nowhere is this more apparent than in the area of financial services, in which the Japanese are currently bringing the same vigor and acumen to bear as they have in the merchandise sector. Partially owing to the rapid appreciation of the yen, Japan's banks overtook those of the United States in terms of international lending assets in early 1986, with Dai-Ichi Kangyo Bank of Tokyo surpassing our own Citibank as the world's largest private financial institution.[48] The Japanese now hold some 8 percent of total shares in U.S. banks and have accumulated controlling interests in a number of Wall Street investment firms. The anticipated internationalization of the yen should boost its value further against the dollar, thereby partly restoring global price competitiveness to American-made goods. Nevertheless, as the yen becomes more prominent as an international currency, the Japanese will benefit in their campaign to capture a larger share of the world's market for financial services.

OUTLOOK AND SUMMARY

At the beginning of 1986, a number of trade analysts expressed the opinion that changing macroeconomic conditions, including favorable exchange rate developments, the convergence of domestic growth rates, and presumed progress in reducing the federal budget deficit, would bring about a reduction

of the American trade deficit within the year.[49] As late as June
1986, Allen Sinai, chief economist at Shearson Lehman Broth-
ers, forecast a 1986 imbalance of under $140 billion.[50] Although
more than eighteen months have elapsed since the U.S. dollar
reached its high point, at the end of the third quarter of 1986,
such predictions seemed overly sanguine. For 1986, the American trade shortfall will probably wind up in a range of $170 bil-
lion to $200 billion, showing little evidence that America is yet
on the road to external balance. The optimists have reacted by
moving their projections ahead, with, for example, Treasury
Secretary James Baker now speaking of a deficit decline to under $100 billion in 1987.[51]

Given that important factors associated with the rise of the
trade deficit, e.g., the strong American dollar, have been weakening for some time, the obvious question is why a turning point
has not yet been firmly established. The orthodox (monetarist)
explanation of the lag lies in the existence of the "J-curve" phenomenon. This analytical device hinges on the premise that dollar devaluation will indeed sharpen the price competitiveness of
our exports and import-competing items, but before this can take
full effect, the price of imports will rise as their volume remains
constant, so that in dollar terms, the trade disequilibrium will
temporarily worsen.

Normally it requires between twelve and eighteen months to
reach a second stage in which improved trade performance is
reflected in our external accounts. But in the present case, a
number of circumstances appear to have delayed the advent of
this phase. The U.S. export bundle includes a large proportion
of "big ticket" capital goods having a longer lead time between
the point at which purchasers make their buying decisions and
the point at which these sales are counted as exports. Foreign
suppliers and American wholesalers/retailers have initially resisted raising import prices to correspond with currency realignments. Anticipating adverse price movements from exchange rates
changes, American middlemen have enlarged their purchases of
imported goods to avoid the full impact of these changes. In the
same manner, expecting an onslaught of protectionist legislation
in reaction to the trade imbalance, foreign suppliers and our own
importers have accelerated the inflow of goods before such re-

strictions can be imposed. Finally, owing to the inordinately lengthy term that trade-related conditions contributing to the deficit were at work, for example, five years of dollar overvaluation, trade balance corrections may be slower in coming than usual. All of this has led conservative trade watchers to predict that some two-and-one-half to three years will be necessary before the J-curve has completed its course.[52]

Against these J-Curve apologetics, the heterodox (structuralist) position rejects the presumption that America's trade performance can be rectified by passively waiting for market corrections to take place. Eschewing the fine calculations of the monetarists, the structuralists have refrained from issuing precise projections about the trade deficit's evolution, but their analyses clearly give a more dismal impression of its future than that outlined in the J-curve scenario. In the end, currency realignments and alterations in domestic growth patterns will not restore international competitiveness to American goods: Only "real" changes in how these products are made will do that. Absent improvements in factors of production and the way in which these resources are managed, the United States will suffer from interminable trade deficits, with only short-term deviations from the downward course in the offing.

Reviewing the chief points covered in this chapter, we find the evidence in support of these respective interpretations can be divided along two dimensions. Focusing on the latitudinal aspect of the imbalance, especially the fact that our bilateral deficits are an across-the-board phenomena, tentatively suggests that America's trade deterioration is primarily the product of adverse macroeconomic conditions; that the monetarists are correct in their reading of it. Turning to its longitudinal facet, the fact that sectoral and industry-specific imbalances have grown progressively worse throughout the 1980s, that is, through significant variations in macroeconomic factors, implies that something of lasting importance is occurring "underneath"; that basic downturns in microeconomic trends are sapping our ability to compete against foreign producers. Any conclusive evaluation of who is right and who is wrong (and to what degree), requires a far more closely detailed examination of these respective viewpoints, and it is to that end that the next chapter of this volume is devoted.

NOTES

1. *New York Times*, August 30, 1986, p. 33.
2. George C. Lodge, *The American Disease* (New York: Alfred A. Knopf, 1984), pp. 16–17.
3. Mary Beth Corbett, "Commerce Department Analysts See Improved Year for U.S. Exports," *Business America*, vol. ix, no. 7 (March 31, 1986), p. 15.
4. Lodge, p. 17.
5. Stephen S. Cohen and John Zysman, "Can America Compete?" *Challenge*, vol. xxviii, no. 3 (May–June 1986), p. 57.
6. Victor B. Bailey and Sara R. Bowden, "Understanding United States Foreign Trade Data," *Business America*, vol. viii, no. 21 (October 14, 1985), p. 4.
7. *U.S. News & World Report*, August 11, 1986, p. 40.
8. *New York Times*, August 30, 1986, p. 1.
9. Preston Martin, "Statement . . . Before the Subcommittee on Economic Stabilization of the Committee on Banking, Finance and Urban Affairs, U.S. House of Representatives, July 18, 1985," *Federal Reserve Bulletin*, vol. lxxi, no. 9 (September 1985), p. 698.
10. *Businessweek*, July 28, 1986, p. 18.
11. Rachel McCulloch, "Point of View: Trade Deficits, Industrial Competitiveness and the Japanese," *California Management Review*, vol. xxvii, no. 2 (Winter 1985), p. 149.
12. Yoshi Tsurumi, "Japan's Challenge to the United States: Industrial Policies and Corporate Strategies," *Revitalizing American Industry: Lessons from Our Competitors*, ed. Milton Hochmuth and William Davidson (Cambridge, Mass.: Ballinger Press, 1985), pp. 39, 45.
13. Joel Dreyfuss, "Japan's Sudden Slowdown," *Fortune*, vol. cxiii, no. 7 (March 31, 1986), p. 23.
14. *Businessweek*, May 19, 1986, p. 30.
15. *New York Times*, September 22, 1986, p. D-6.
16. C. Fred Bergstein, "The U.S.–Japan Trade Imbroglio," *Challenge*, vol. xxviii, no. 3 (July–August 1985), p. 15.
17. McCulloch, p. 143.
18. *New York Times*, April 22, 1986, p. A-31.
19. Lawrence Minard, "Noah's Ark, Anyone?" *Forbes*, vol. cxxxvi, no. 4 (August 12, 1985), p. 76.
20. Vincent Reinhart, "Macroeconomic Influences on the U.S.–Japan Trade Imbalance," *Federal Reserve Bank of New York*, vol. xi, no. 1 (Spring 1986), p. 7.

21. *New York Times*, July 3, 1986, p. D-7.

22. *New York Times*, September 22, 1986, p. D-6.

23. Bruce Stokes, "Korea: Relations Worsen," *National Journal*, vol. xviii, no. 18 (April 5, 1986), p. 814.

24. Ibid., p. 815.

25. *Businessweek*, July 28, 1986, p. 25.

26. David A. Heenan, "Building Industrial Cooperation Through Japanese Strategies," *Business Horizons*, vol, xxviii, no. 6 (November–December 1985), pp. 10–11.

27. Bruce R. Scott, "Can Industry Survive the Welfare State?" *Harvard Business Review*, vol. lx, no. 5 (September–October 1982), p. 72.

28. Andrew Tanzer, "The Trouble with Merchantilism," *Forbes*, vol. cxxxviii, no. 3 (August 11, 1986), p. 36.

29. *Businessweek*, August 11, 1986, p. 41.

30. *Businessweek*, July 28, 1986, p. 25.

31. *New York Times*, September 15, 1986, p. A-14.

32. "U.S. Trade Outlook," *Business America*, vol. ix, no. 6 (March 17, 1986), p. 4.

33. Robert Z. Lawrence, "The Myth of U.S. Deindustrialization," *Challenge*, vol. xxvi, no. 5 (November–December 1983), p. 21.

34. Henry Eason, "Keeping the Trade Deficit in the Right Perspective," *Nation's Business*, vol. lxxii, no. 10 (October 1984), p. 56.

35. Charles L. Schultze, "Industrial Policy: A Dissent," *Brookings Review*, vol. ii, no. 1 (Fall 1983), p. 5.

36. *Business America*, "U.S. Trade Outlook," p. 3.

37. *Businessweek*, August 18, 1986, p. 63.

38. N. B. Hannay and Lowell W. Steele, "Technology and Trade: A Study of U.S. Competitiveness in Seven Industries," *Research Management*, vol. xxix, no. 1 (January–February 1986), p. 21.

39. Robert A. Johnson, "U.S. International Transaction in 1985," *Federal Reserve Bulletin*, vol. lxxii, no. 5 (May 1986), p. 290.

40. *New York Times*, July 13, 1986, p. F-6.

41. *Business America*, "U.S. Trade Outlook," p. 4.

42. *New York Times*, August 30, 1986, p. 33.

43. Edwin A. Finn, "Good Medicine, Too Few Patients," *Forbes*, vol. cxxxvii, no. 7 (April 7, 1986), p. 31.

44. *U.S. News and World Report*, August 11, 1986, p. 41.

45. *New York Times*, July 31, 1986, p. D-7.

46. Richard N. Cooper, "Dealing with the Trade Deficit in a Floating Rate System," *Brookings Papers on Economic Activity*, no. 1 (1986), p. 203.

47. *New York Times*, September 14, 1986, p. F-4.

48. *New York Times*, August 7, 1986, p. D-4.
49. *Johnson*, p. 287.
50. *New York Times*, June 8, 1986, p. D-1.
51. *Businessweek*, June 9, 1986, p. 3.
52. *Nation's Business*, June 1986, p. 10.

2

THE ORIGINS OF THE TRADE DEFICIT

THE MONETARIST POSITION

From the monetarist standpoint, the U.S. trade deficit of the 1980s is grounded in those broad macroeconomic factors which form the basic "environment" or "context" in which trade takes place. The two principal forces which have caused the trade imbalance are the longstanding overvaluation of the dollar and the inordinately high rate of growth in the American domestic economy relative to those of other nations. At bottom, both of these factors are monetary, as opposed to "real," in nature. This is virtually self-evident in the case of currency values, but, from the monetarist perspective, it is equally true of output growth. The central tenet of monetarism is that, in the long run, growth of output occurs in direct correlation with the growth of an economy's money/credit supply. The strong spurt of GNP growth posted by the United States in 1983 and 1984 was the result of an overrapid expansion in monetary aggregates. This unwarranted growth was created by two interrelated streams: (a) a "loose" policy on the part of the Federal Reserve Board aiming to accommodate the federal government fiscal deficits while maintaining private investment growth; and (b) an inflow of foreign capital into U.S. assets induced by the existence of comparatively high-yield, low-risk investment opportunities in the United States.

Delving deeper, it is excess domestic demand, that is, consumption and credit demand beyond what can be sustained through internal production, that is the ultimate source of those monetary factors which have generated the trade deficit. Siphoning off a large portion of potential national savings, excess demand has created an investment gap within the United States, with an accommodationist monetary policy *and* an inflow of foreign capital rushing in to fill the vacuum. Certain other forces, for instance, impediments to the workings of market mechanism in the form of tax, antitrust and regulatory regimes, have played a marginal role in the emergence of the American trade deficit. But the root cause is public and private deficit expenditure; and so, the monetarist understanding of the trade imbalance is a tightly unified conception revolving around excessive aggregate demand.

Perhaps the most straightforward way of unraveling the monetarist version of the trade deficit's origins is to begin with international exchange rates. The relative value of a nation's currency exerts a direct and powerful influence upon its trade performance. When a country's currency appreciates relative to those of other major trading nations, the price of its exports in foreign markets tends to rise in local currency terms. Consequently, the volume of its exports is reduced as their price competitiveness is blunted. Obversely (and more significantly in the case of the American trade imbalance), the corresponding depreciation of foreign currencies decreases prices on their exports in local currency terms; hence, the volume of their exports to the markets of the appreciating currency economy (and third-country markets) tends to increase as they are lent a price advantage over domestically produced goods.

While the movement of exchange values over time can be computed with a fair degree of accuracy, such calculations will vary with (a) the inclusion or exclusion of different foreign currencies in the "basket" against which a specific national currency is measured, and (b) the method used to adjust for domestic price inflation within both the economy of the currency being measured and those of the currencies included in the basket as yardsticks. Returning to Table 1 (page 8), we observe that between the third quarter of 1980 and the first quarter of 1985 the

U.S. dollar appreciated some 75 percent against those of the G-10 (major industrial) nations when adjusted for domestic price movements through the methods of the Federal Reserve. Alternatively, Morgan Guaranty analysts using a broader basket of currencies (those of the G-10 nations *and* those of five developing countries having large trade volumes with the United States) and a different inflation-adjustment method, report a dollar appreciation of only 30 percent over the same period.[1] This disparity aside, Table 1 reveals two unmistakable trends: (1) the steep rise of the dollar relative to other major trading currencies over a span of nearly five years, and (2) a direct correspondence between this appreciation and increased import penetration of the American economy.

How important is the overvalued dollar as a causal factor in the emergence of the American trade deficit? In the words of former Chairwoman of the U.S. International Trade Commission Paula Stern: "Overall, the most powerful force in determining America's laggard competitiveness performance in recent years has been the increase in the value of the dollar against other world currencies."[2] In support of this statement, Stern cites a study conducted by the Federal Reserve Board that attributes 87 percent of the increase in the total U.S. trade deficit between 1980 and 1984 to the superdollar.[3] Because of the interconnections between exchange and growth rates, other researchers, distinguishing between them for analytical purposes, ascribe a more modest role to dollar overvaluation as the source of the trade deficit. For example, Vincent Reinhart estimates that about one-third of the growth in the bilateral trade deficit between the United States and Japan during the 1980 to early 1985 period was the product of dollar/yen exchange rates, with another 40 percent owing to growth rate differentials.[4] Whether combined with growth rates or treated distinctly, the strength of the dollar against Western European and Japanese currencies in the first half of the 1980s was *a* major, if not *the* major, proximate cause of the American trade imbalance, according to the monetarist argument.

At this juncture, the reader may be puzzled by a seeming paradox. He may well ask: Shouldn't the relative value of a national currency reflect the underlying state of its economy, es-

pecially its international competitiveness, and, if so, why did the
dollar rise while America's international accounts were deteriorating? The point is well taken, and, in fact, in the long term,
exchange rate movements should mirror current and prospective
trends in the fundamental soundness of different economies as
demonstrated by the depreciation of the dollar since February
1985. In the short run, however, other forces can intervene to
delay exchange rate adjustment. Most critically, it is the enormous expansion of "autonomous" international capital flows, i.e.,
cross-border movements of money not directly tied to exist-
ing/future real investment, which explains the prolonged irrela-
tion between the dollar's value and America's trade performance.

The large overlay of portfolio capital movements upon money
flows in support of trade and direct investment exerts a determining influence upon exchange rates in the near term. The magnitude of this expansion is apparent when we consider that between 1979 and 1984, total world exports increased in value from
$1.5 trillion to $1.8 trillion, but, at the same time, foreign exchange trading grew from $17.5 trillion a year to $35 trillion.[5]
The upshot of this rise in speculative capital flows is that the
criteria for shifting among investment markets and currencies
"now frequently reflects fluctuations in interest rates on financial instruments or altered appraisals of the exchange rate attrac-
tions of different currencies, rather than the attraction of new
opportunities for real investment."[6] In a world of high capital
mobility, money moves in and out of different currencies based
on differential rates of return and anticipated changes in foreign
exchange values. Indeed, beyond any question, the direct "cause"
of the American trade deficit is an influx of foreign capital which
has, in effect, financed our overconsumption of foreign goods.
In a sense, we have experienced an erosion in our international
competitiveness because the in-migration of world capital to the
dollar has accommodated American import purchases at the cost
of further stifling the price competitiveness of American goods
at home and abroad. Hence, while a decline in the dollar was
inevitable given the downturn in the fundamental well-being of
the American economy, for a sustained period, international
portfolio capital movements held the dollar up, enabling the United

States to forestall the adjustment impact of corrective foreign exchange realignments.

The motive behind the surge of foreign capital into the United States was not to perversely generate trade surpluses with America: It was simply the rational choice of Japanese and Western European investors to maximize their returns by shifting into dollar-denominated assets. During the early 1980s, the conjunction of a tight, nonaccommodationist Federal Reserve Board policy with a wildly expansionary federal govenment fiscal policy squeezed domestic credit markets, causing both nominal (face) and "real" (inflation-adjusted) interest rates to reach very high levels. Following an austere, anti-inflationary course, the Federal Reserve Bank's discount rate to commercial banks ranged between 11 percent and 13.5 percent, leading to prime rates on loans from these institutions of between 14.5 percent and 19 percent.[7] Competing with high interest federal debt issues for available savings, commercial banks were compelled to raise deposit rates in order to attract private savings. By the same token, since the discount rates of central banks in our chief trading rivals were about one-half our own,[8] and since fiscal austerity on the part of their governments meant less intense competition for private savings, foreign banks were able to attract sufficient indigenous savings at much lower deposit rates.

About mid-1983, the U.S. Federal Reserve Board shifted gears as its inflation fears were pushed to the side and stimulating domestic economic growth became its primary mission. Discount rates were progressively lowered to 5.5 percent by mid-1986; the prime rate dropped to a range of 7 percent to 8 percent, and deposit rates were cut to less than half their 1981 peak. At the same time, however, the governments of our chief trade competitors followed suit by cutting their own discount rates (eventually leading to a reduction of rates offered to savers/investors in their economies), while the demand for credit in the United States remained strong. Thus, despite the reversal in the Fed's policy, over the term 1981 to 1985 real U.S. interest rates on bank deposits, public and private bonds, etc., remained remarkably constant at between 275 and 400 basis points above those available in Japan and West Germany.

According to the Organization for Economic Cooperation and

Development (OECD), since the fourth quarter of 1984, the interest rate differential between the United States and Japan/West Germany has narrowed somewhat. Between September 1985 and June 1986, short-term U.S. interest rates declined from 7.5 percent to 6.5 percent, long-term rates dropping from 10.5 percent to 8.0 percent. Over the same period Bundesbank discount rate cuts permitted West German institutions to reduce long-term interest rates from 6.5 percent to 6.1 percent (short-term rates remaining stable at 4.5 percent), while Japan's savers/investors have watched long-term yields decline from 5.8 percent to 5.0 percent and short-term rates drop from 6.2 percent to 4.6 percent.[9] In other words, American interest-bearing assets continue to be highly attractive to the Germans and Japanese because they have continued to produce yields well above those available in their home economies, albeit with a narrowing differential of late. It should be noted in passing that yields on British, French, and Canadian interest-paying instruments have been and still are *above* those offered by American public and private bodies, and, hence, very little capital inflow has been recorded from these countries into the United States. Nevertheless, Japanese and West German investors still have ample reason to convert their yen and deutsche mark savings into dollars in order to take advantage of the spread between what they can earn in their own countries and what they can realize by acquiring U.S. paper.

Several ancillary factors have worked to keep American interest rates comparatively high and pave the way for the inrush of foreign money which has allowed the United States to incur its enormous trade deficits. As one of the principal planks of the Reagan administration's "supply side" economics, 1981 and 1982 tax legislation offered generous write-offs on new investment and plant/equipment depreciation.[10] This, in turn, created a capital spending boom in the United States with an attendant upward pressure on interest rates. The overall reduction in corporate tax burdens embodied in these tax reform measures, moreover, increased returns to capital on U.S. investments, making American equities even more attractive to foreigners.[11] More pointedly, in 1983 the U.S. Congress opened the floodgates for foreign capital inflows even further by rescinding withholding tax on interest payments to foreign investors,[12] leaving its critics to complain that the government was ushering in a period of American external debt and perpetuating the trade imbalance by tailoring U.S. investments to foreign tastes.[13]

While all of these forces were significant in maintaining a positive interest rate differential between America and its main commercial rivals, the strongest factor accounting for interest rates favoring U.S. assets was, and is, the extraordinary demand for credit resulting from perennial federal budget deficits. It has been estimated that a balanced central government budget in 1984 would have reduced interest rates on one-year U.S. Treasury bills by more than 200 basis points in that year,[14] and that a $100 billion reduction in the federal budget deficit for 1985 would have led long-term interest rates to decline by 160 basis points.[15]

Having followed a circuitous route, we now confront the main culprit in the monetarist understanding of the emergence of the American trade imbalance, excess domestic demand most clearly manifest in yearly federal govenment outlays far beyond annual revenues. Indeed, due to the close historical parallels between them, the budget and trade deficits are often referred to as "twins." Quite plainly, "as the (federal government) budget deficit moved out of its historical range to record levels, so did the U.S. deficit on merchandise trade."[16]

We need not recount the well-worn tale of the federal government's growing fiscal profligacy, but a few broad observations can underscore its magnitude. In 1979, all levels of American government (state and local included) registered a budget *surplus* equivalent to 0.6 percent of U.S. GNP. By 1985 (even as state and local governments remained in the black), the total public *deficit* amounted to 4.5 percent of national output.[17] In 1985, the federal government received $734 billion in revenues, but it spent $946 billion, creating a yearly deficit of $212.3 billion, a record sure to be overtaken in 1986. These figures pale when compared to the accumulated national public debt of $2.11 trillion at mid-1986 (cash basis),[18] which has been alternatively figured at $3.8 trillion (accrual basis).[19] Since even the most patriotic citizens are not willing to loan their government funds without receiving a return on investment, all of this accreted debt must be serviced, causing real American interest rates to stay at historically high levels. Some of the interest-raising effect of this heap of internal public debt has been dampened by the Fed's accommodationist stance. But rapid growth in the money supply risks future domestic price inflation and, in turn, the need for higher interest rates to compensate savers for its erosive effects. Since high American interest rates push the value of the dollar upward, in spite of its depreciation since February 1985, Michael Hutchinson and Adrian Throop assert that, "as long as U.S. structural budget deficits remain large relative to those abroad, the real value of the dollar should remain substantially above its pre-1980 level."[20] Indeed, Richard Cooper has put the matter even more directly by asserting that if the federal budget deficit in 1984 had been $100 billion lower than it was, the United States "would have produced a healthy and not abnormal trade surplus in goods and services of about 0.5 percent of GNP."[21]

The impact of the federal deficit on our trade performance during the 1980s has often been cited by free trade advocates as an alternative explanation to the protectionist denunciation of unfair practices on the part of our main competitors. Nevertheless, Senator John Danforth, chairman of the Trade Sub-Committee of the Senate Finance Committee, and one of the most vehement critics of unfair foreign trade tactics, has frankly admitted that: "There is no change in the trade laws which will reduce the trade deficit so long as we run the Federal budget deficits that we have."[22]

Although massive federal budget deficits represent the most visible source of positive interest rate differentials holding up a severely overvalued dollar, in identifying aggregate domestic demand as the cause of America's trade woes, the monetarist "buck" does not stop exclusively at the door of government. For one, American corporations and private citizens have been closely mimicking the fiscal imprudence of their government. According to Federal Reserve figures, in 1986 the public debt of the United States stood at $1.7 trillion (an extremely conservative estimate), up from $750 billion in 1978, but American *private* debt was calculated at $7 trillion in 1986, compared with $3.25 trillion eight years before.[23] After decades in which total public/private debt approximated 160 percent of annual GNP, since 1982 total debt has bounded to over 200 percent of yearly national output.[24] Hence, corporations and individuals have gorged themselves with debt at about the same rate as the federal government, with identical consequences for interest rates, exchange values, and the trade deficit.

From a slightly different angle, the monetarist position maintains that, "roughly speaking, current trade deficits have their roots in the recent fall of total U.S. savings."[25] Part and parcel with the rise of private debt there has been a noticeable downturn in the propensity of the American public to save.[26] At least hypothetically, had U.S. private savings continued at the +10 percent of GNP rate which they achieved in the early 1970s, both our debt and investment needs *could* have been met through internal savings, i.e., without an inflow of foreign capital.

As depicted in Table 3, two trends are apparent. First, yearly net private savings as a percentage of the country's GNP display a broad contraction, with 1980s average annual rates being well below those of the 1970s. We get some idea of just how low private savings in the United States have been when we compare them to those of our trade competitors. Placing U.S. household savings at 6.3 percent of GNP in 1984, Lawrence Minard cites corresponding rates of 17.7 percent and 11.5 percent for Japan and West Germany respectively.[27] Basil Caplan's estimate of Japanese national savings in 1985 (18 percent) in contrast to American national savings (2.1 percent) gives us an even more alarming picture of the gulf between U.S. savings rates and those of our chief trade nemesis.[28] Nor is a higher propensity to save confined to industrialized trade competitors. In 1985, for instance, Taiwan enjoyed the highest national savings rate in the world, amounting to 32 percent of its GNP.[29]

The second trend evident in Table 3 is that, given a low and generally declining rate of private savings, the federal government's budget deficits absorb a far greater proportion of private savings than do the relatively modest fiscal deficits of Japan and West Germany. John Cuddy informs us that from 1982 onward, while total U.S. public deficits amounted to between 60 percent and 70 percent of available private savings, in Japan, government claims were between 25 percent and 30 percent of net private savings, while those of the principal European Economic Community nations (West Germany, France, the United King-

Table 3
United States Savings Rates, 1973–1985 (as percentages of U.S. GNP)

Year	Net Private Saving	Government Saving	Net National Saving
1973	10.1	0.6	10.8
1974	8.8	-0.3	8.4
1975	9.9	-4.5	5.4
1976	8.9	-2.4	6.5
1977	8.6	-1.1	7.5
1978	8.9	-0.0	8.8
1979	8.0	0.5	8.5
1980	7.2	-1.4	5.8
1981	7.5	-1.1	6.4
1982	6.3	-4.0	2.3
1983	6.7	-4.4	2.3
1984	8.2	-3.2	4.9
1985	7.3	-3.9	3.4

Source: *Conference Board Research Bulletin*, no. 198
(1986), p. 24.

dom, and Italy) took an average 40 percent to 50 percent of private savings.[30] Quite obviously, with private savings low and the
lion's share of these being consumed by federal budget deficits,
America's remaining national savings rate becomes negligible,
amounting to but 1.5 percent of GNP during one month in early
1986.[31] With available savings so low, private investment must
be curtailed absent an inflow from abroad. Thus, an "investment
gap" results featuring high interest rates and inadequate capital
formation as the private sector is crowded out of credit markets
by public borrowing.[32] It is this investment chasm which has

been filled by foreign investors as they have sent their savings into both the private and the public sectors of the American economy, with, for instance, Japanese investors now holding some $100 billion in U.S. government obligations.[33]

In itself, the federal government's spendthrift ways are a necessary, but not a sufficient, cause of the exchange rate/interest rate repression of our trade performance: Had private domestic savings rates been greater or the private demand for credit lower, the global price competitiveness of American goods and services would not have suffered as much. Federal budget deficits, corporate/individual debt and declining/inadequate private savings, then, are all "heads" of the same hydra to the monetarist, that is, consumption levels unmatched by the value of national output leading to the external imbalance of the trade deficit.[34]

Why do Americans save proportionately less than, for example, their Japanese counterparts? Part of the reason is deeply embedded in differences of national culture and character, and, as such, far removed from the field of monetarist analysis. Nonetheless, there are objective economic forces that have served to magnify variations in the savings/consumption behavior of the two countries.

In the case of Japan, strong incentives to save have been built into the domestic economy. The Japanese income tax system includes extremely favorable treatment of interest earnings from private savings. Through Japan's postal savings system, individual citizens can accumulate some $60,000 in their accounts free of levies on interest.[35] Because of the comparatively underdeveloped extent of their social security programs and the fact that pensions from private employers are typically quite modest, the Japanese save, in effect, because they must provide for themselves.[36] In complementary fashion, the Japanese tax regime strongly discourages the use of consumer credit.[37] Annual income tax deductions on mortgage interest are limited to $1,100, while interest payments on consumer credit are completely nondeductible.[38]

In sharp relief to this savings-biased system, tax provisions in the United States inhibit private savings by imposing relatively high rate burdens on interest and dividend earnings. The advanced American social safety net permits individuals to shift their savings needs (retirement, medical expenses, etc.) to government and employers.[39] Worse, the federal income tax code effectively rewards consumer debt by granting liberal interest payment deductions on everything from home mortgages to appliances purchased with credit cards. Consequently, in direct contrast to Japan, the American welfare state, with its array of social entitlements and its unabashed promotion of consumerism, maintains powerful disincentives to save.

The second major factor in the monetarist diagnosis of the U.S. trade deficit is that of differences in rates of domestic economic growth. As previously indicated, distinguishing between the "exchange rate effect" and the "growth differential effect" upon America's deteriorating trade account is a difficult conceptual task: The same fundamental force, excess consumption, which led to an overvalued dollar also contributed to the overheating of the American economy. Nevertheless, for expository purposes, such a distinction can be made, and, for political purposes, it certainly has been made. With regard to the latter, the Reagan administration has seized upon the growth differential aspect of the monetarist position as a means of rationalizing the growth of the trade imbalance. Thus, President Reagan has declared that "The trade deficit has grown because economic difficulties abroad have persisted while the United States has been more successful in utilizing our economic opportunities."[40]

The core of this assertion is that faster GNP growth, and hence per capita income growth, during the 1983–1984 U.S. recovery stimulated high levels of import consumption and created those financial opportunities that attracted foreign capital into the American economy. Concurrently, so the "official line" goes, comparatively slow growth in the economies of our main trading partners repressed demand for exports from the United States and prompted foreign savers to look to America for investment growth.[41] Until September 1985, the administration also subsumed the "exchange rate effect" into this polemical version of the trade deficit, contending that the strong dollar was simply a reflection of the robust state of the domestic economy. Although this facet of the argument has since been yanked, the rose-colored "growth differential effect" has remained the Reagan administration's pet justification for the trade imbalance. As any monetarist would be quick to point out, what this disingenuous explanation fails to acknowledge is that our faster rate of GNP growth was debt-led, being supported by an imprudent expansion of the money supply and an influx of debt-crediting foreign capital.

Returning again to Table 1 (on page 8) even without the benefit of comparisons with other economies, it is evident that the growth of import penetration in both capital and consumer goods was strongest during the period when real U.S. output growth was most rapid, i.e., from the second quarter of 1983 through the final quarter of 1984. Alluding to the influence of divergent growth/per capita income growth rates on the U.S.–Japan bilateral trade imbalance, Jeffrey Bergstrand informs us:

In 1983, U.S. and Japanese real GNP grew at 3.7 percent and 3.2 percent rates respectively (year-over-year). In 1984, the U.S. grew at a 6.8 percent rate while Japan grew by 5.1 percent. This growth rate differential can partly explain why U.S. imports from Japan grew at a faster rate than Japanese imports from the United States.[42]

While these disparities in growth rates are not large in absolute terms, given that Japanese GNP growth was about twice that of the United States during the three decades before 1980, the subsequent convergence in the 1980s was, in fact, extreme. When Japan's real output growth maintained its long-standing pace of over 6 percent annually and the United States conformed to its historical norm of 3 percent yearly growth, the U.S.–Japan trade balance approximated equilibrium. Subsequently, when the Japanese growth rate began to slow toward the American pace at the end of the 1970s, Japanese exports to the United States gained momentum before the pronounced takeoff of 1983/1984. According to Vincent Reinhart, the narrowing of the U.S.–Japan growth rate differential in the 1980s was responsible for 40 percent of the increase in America's trade deficit with Japan between 1980 and early 1985.[43] In short, America's faster domestic expansion translated into higher per capita income, and a large portion of this disposable cash was devoted to purchases of Japanese imports.

This same basic pattern of domestic growth in the United States outstripping domestic growth in the economies of our principal trading partners can be discerned in Western Europe, Canada, and the developing countries of Latin America. Indeed, as an outcome of the recessionary effects of the second oil shock and continued anti-inflationary policies, collective real GNP growth in Western Europe between 1981 and 1984 averaged a mere 1.5 percent a year.[44] 1985 and the first half of 1986 saw a rebound in Western European output expansion to the 2.5 percent to 3 percent range, but the preoccupation of European fiscal/monetary authorities with rekindling price inflation has caused them to keep a tight rein on potential fiscal/monetary stimuli.[45] As to Canada, the government of Prime Minister Brian Mulroney has a far better "excuse" for keeping a lid on domestic growth: Past fiscal excesses have left Canada with an internal public debt larger than that of the United States when measured as a percentage of annual GNP. In Latin America, increases in output/per capita income, and, above all, imports of dollar-denominated goods, have been held back as stringent adjustment programs to deal with external debts have been applied.[46] With sporadic interruptions, growth in South Korea and Taiwan has moved along at a rapid clip. Unfortunately, the United States has not enjoyed an export surge to either of these Asian NICs due to the small size of their domestic markets.

Turning from the underlying cause of weak import demand abroad, that is, growth rate differentials, to an analysis of foreign import demand per se, a controversial issue emerges. To those critics of foreign trading practices, the meager amount of American goods coming to Japan, and, to a lesser extent, European expenditures on American wares, is *prima facie* evidence that these commercial rivals have resorted to trade barriers that have artificially constricted American exports into their markets. As I shall shortly detail, the monetarist school categorically rejects this assertion, and ascribes lagging import growth in the economies of our chief trading partners to exchange rates and growth rate differentials. Assuming, for the moment, that the monetarists are substantially correct on this point, the impact of the growth slowdown in Japan upon imports from the United States and elsewhere has been profound. In 1981, a total of $142.9 billion in goods from all sources was imported into

Japan: By 1985, total imports had *declined* to $136.9 billion. In analogous fashion, while 1981 West German imports from all sources were valued at $163.9 billion, 1985's import tally was $160.3 billion. Part of the explanation for this absolute decline lies in reduced oil-import volumes/prices for these nations. Nonetheless, in the case of Japan, imports of manufactured items have remained unchanged during the 1980s at a miniscule 2.5 percent of national output.[47] Hence, impediments to imports apart, relatively slow GNP/per capita income growth in the 1980s on the part of some of our main export outlet economies appears to have stymied the expansion of American sales in these markets.

We cannot leave the growth rate differential effect without a reiteration and a qualification. First, from the monetarist viewpoint, it must be emphasized, rapid American growth and associated import increases were fueled by rising levels of internal and external debt. Thus, while the growth rate differential can help to explain America's eroding trade performance, it can by no means act as an apology for it. As importantly, it was primarily the boost given to imports by strong GNP growth in the United States, and only secondarily the dampening of American exports from slow growth abroad, which appears to be the critical side of the growth rate differential equation for the trade imbalance. For example, Reinhart notes that U.S. imports of Japanese goods are three times more sensitive to domestic income growth than Japanese imports of American products. This implies that "Japan's real income must grow nearly three times the U.S. rate to maintain balanced increases in export and import volumes."[48] In line with this finding, a recent study commissioned by the International Monetary Fund estimated that an increase of one percentage point in German and Japanese growth would reduce the U.S. trade deficit by a small $9 billion to $12 billion in any given year.[49] The hard lesson highlighted by these analyses is that overrapid American domestic growth, *not* desultory GNP gains abroad, is the critical element of the growth rate differential's impact on the U.S. trade deficit.

Beyond the adverse workings of exchange rates and domestic growth patterns, the monetarist explanation of the trade imbalance's origins has little more to say. There are, however, a handful of policy factors that have played an auxiliary role in the decline of America's trade performance to the extent that they have interfered with the free operation of market forces. Chief among these are those tax, antitrust, and regulatory policies that have distorted the allocation of our domestic resources and imposed added burdens upon American producers compared to their foreign counterparts.

We have already touched upon one of these market impediments in the form of a U.S. tax system which actively favors private consumption and inhibits savings, investment, and work.[50] There are additional aspects of the American tax regime that have seriously handicapped American industry and which the monetarists would undoubtedly alter if given the opportunity to do so. For instance, the United States imposes a fairly stiff tax on capital gains, thereby discouraging investment, particularly in high-risk new ventures, while the Japanese tax code includes no corresponding levy.[51] The U.S. government displays a far greater dependence upon corporate income taxes as a source of revenue than, for instance, West European governments that rely more heavily on value-added taxes.[52] As to the sweeping tax reform package passed by Congress in 1986, the monetarists certainly applaud its reduction of top tax rates on both corporations and individuals, and they are even more enthusiastic about its elimination of distortionary deductions and loopholes. Nonetheless, for the monetarists, the new tax law is a mixed blessing. Aside from the fact that it does nothing to bring revenues into line with federal expenditures, by shifting some $120 billion of the federal tax burden from individuals to business over a five-year period,[53] the Achilles heel of the new tax bill, from the monetarist viewpoint, is that it creates a further bias toward consumption and away from productive investment.

The monetarists are similarly divided when it comes to U.S. antitrust provisions. Although their ostensible purpose is to promote free market competition within the United States (a truly noble goal to monetarists), the means employed to achieve this purpose, i.e., government antitrust intervention, runs directly contrary to monetarist precepts. As George Cabot Lodge and William Crom assert: "Past antitrust standards have arguably deterred export activities, discouraged industry cooperation and failed to adequately reflect the impact of foreign competition when evaluating combinations of domestic companies seeking economies of scale.''[54] To the degree to which they have constrained the workings of the marketplace, and, more specifically, impinged upon the activities of export/import-competing enterprises, our trust-busting regulations have had an unwarranted, negative influence on America's trade record insofar as the monetarists are concerned.

Lastly, the monetarists have no qualms whatsoever about the abrasive impact of the American government's regulatory apparatus upon domestic business confronting strident foreign competition. Federal and state agencies engage in a wide variety of regulatory enforcement activities (environmental laws, occupational safety and health codes, consumer protection shields, etc.) which impose a cost burden on American business that is in many cases far heavier than that borne by foreign producers. Conforming to these dictates entails large capital expenditures, a diversion of managerial attention, reams of paperwork, and, as with safety, energy, and pollution control requirements on American automobiles, compulsory costs which must be passed down to consumers.[55] In their multi-industry competitiveness study, the National Academy of Engineering commented that American pharmaceutical manufacturers are subject to regulatory costs and delays that are significantly higher than those abroad (an average of eight years between application for Food and Drug Administration approval of new drugs and their certification by the F.D.A.) and that they are the *most significant factor* responsible for the recent loss of American shares in global drug markets.[56] To the extent that it impedes market forces, the nation's regulatory machinery is a strong hindrance from the monetarist viewpoint; thus, it follows that to the extent that it affects export/import competing businesses, it has contributed, albeit marginally, to the U.S. trade deficit.

To this juncture, I have been dealing with the monetarist understanding of the trade imbalance's origins in purely affirmative terms, that is, by covering those factors that the monetarists identify as its root causes. Before moving to consideration of the structuralist version of the trade deficit's origins, I will briefly

deviate from this course by examining a set of factors—protectionist-mercantilist policies on the part of our trade competitors—which monetarism steadfastly *rejects* as a source of the
trade deficit. Admittedly, approaching this topic under the head-
ing of the monetarist analysis may appear incongruous. Nonetheless, the refutation of the "foreign protectionism" argument
is a major and integral plank of the monetarist position; thus,
there is a rationale for, and a need for, bringing it up at this
point.

Because I plan to cover the alleged influence of "unfair" foreign trade policies on America's trade account in greater detail
elsewhere in this chapter, only a brief synposis of the most basic
charges against these policies is necessary here. Speaking, inevitably, of Japan, Senator Danforth has propounded that "no
other nation contributes so little to the open trading system of
the world in proportion to what it gains."[57] When we examine
Japan's schedule of import duties, Danforth's characterization
seems completely unfounded. As its trade officials have end-
lessly pointed out, Japan's tariffs on manufactured imports are
the lowest among all of the major industrial nations.[58] Comply-
ing with Tokyo Round (1980) negotiations, Japan has cut its tariffs on manufactured goods to an average of 2.9 percent, between 1.5 percentage points and 4 percentage points below those
of the United States, Canada, and Western Europe.[59] Since other
countries with whom the United States has posted large bilateral
trade deficits, notably South Korea and Taiwan, have much higher
duty rates, singling out Japan for its protectionist policies seems
absurd.

As Japan's critics are quick to retort, however, the real problem is not overt tariffs, but (a) a wide network of nontariff barriers to imports and (b) an elaborate program of export subsidies
which lend Japanese goods an unfair advantage in foreign markets. Taking the first part of this indictment into consideration,
it is charged that through licensing procedures, government procurement policies, and the informal rigidities of its closed distribution systems, Japanese officials and commercial intermediaries effectively constrict American sales of goods and services
in Japan. Although the precise effect of Japan's nontariff bar-

riers is difficult to measure[60] (hence their alternative designation as "intangibles"), vociferous "Japan bashers" claim that they are a major causal factor in the growth of America's bilateral imbalance with the Japanese.

The monetarist rebuttal of the "intangible barriers" impact on the central U.S.–Japan bilateral trade relation has two parts. First, those empirical studies of Japanese nontariff impediments to U.S. goods which have been published come to the same general conclusion: that a full opening of the Japanese economy would lead to increased American sales there by some $5 billion[61] to $7 billion.[62] Consequently, as Dorothy Christelow has summarized it, the long-term U.S. export gain from the hypothetical removal of Japanese nontariff barriers is "too small to suggest that intangible barriers are the primary or even a major source of Japan's external trade surpluses,"[63] with America and other economies. Second, as I mentioned in Chapter 1, regrettably, from the monetarist perspective, the United States has erected its own nontariff barriers against Japanese goods, especially the OMAs governing auto, steel, textiles, etc. Were complete trade liberalization to occur on both sides, then, in all likelihood the U.S.–Japan bilateral imbalance would increase.[64]

As to the next count in this bill of particulars, the charge that foreign governments, most prominently Japan, unfairly subsidize their export industries, enabling them to dump goods in American markets at low cost and thereby wrest market shares from domestic producers, the monetarist refutation is again twofold. First, as McCulloch reminds us, "dumping . . . as defined in U.S. statutes is a normal business practice of most firms with substantial fixed costs and fluctuating demand—including our own firms in cyclical industries."[65] If foreign suppliers price their exports to the United States below their production cost, that is their free market prerogative.

Less dogmatically, as reported by Norman Fiekle in his study of the price behavior of Japanese, West German, and Canadian imports to the United States between 1980 and early 1985, two empirical points call into question the validity of the foreign dumping argument. First, in the case of all imports from these three nations, the degree to which their prices in the United States declined over this term was smaller than the extent to which their currencies simultaneously depreciated against the American dollar. This finding is clearly inconsistent with the view that these governments push their exports by broadly subsidizing or surpressing export prices.[66] Second, in the case of threatening imports (autos, steel, textiles, etc.) purported to have been targeted at the United States by the governments of Japan, West Germany, and Canada, their actual prices showed no deviation from the pattern of declines equal to or less than that which would be expected on the basis of currency value changes.[67] Consequently, the monetarists reject the notion that competitive price-cutting is somehow objectionable when national borders are crossed, and, at the same time, they marshal evidence to show that widespread dumping has not, in fact, occurred.

The last monetarist argument against foreign protectionism as the cause of America's trade deficit is by far the broadest (encompassing tariffs, nontariff barriers, and subsidies) and the most convincing. It rests on an observation advanced, *inter alia*, by Robert Lawrence and Robert Litan, who point out that "the trading system is no more unfair to the United States (in 1985) than it was in 1981 when the United States enjoyed a positive trade balance in manufactured goods."[68] Assuming, for the sake of argument, that our trade competitors do engage in protectionist-mercantilist policies of various degrees of subtlety, there is no evidence that they are now more protectionist than in 1980 when the United States registered surpluses or modest deficits against them.[69] In fact, from all appearances, Japan, and to a lesser extent Western Europe, have partially dismantled such trade barriers against American goods as were in place at the beginning in the 1980s, while the United States, through its "voluntary restraint" programs, has raised its protectionist walls. This simple, common sense argument thoroughly punctures the unfair foreign trade policy rationalization of the U.S. trade deficits. As such, it underscores a thread that runs throughout the monetarist analysis of the trade imbalance's origins, that the fault and the responsibility for the trade deficit is grounded in the United States itself and not elsewhere.

THE STRUCTURALIST POSITION: PART I

Tightly woven and constructed with the analytical rigor of a geometric proof, the monetarist interpretation of the origins of the U.S. trade deficit leaves us with the impression that nothing remains to be said on the matter. In fact, the alternative structuralist argument has much to tell us about the source of the American trade imbalance apart from exchange rate movements and growth rate differentials. The structuralist version of the trade deficit's causes focuses on the "content," as opposed to the "context," of our trade performance. It examines microeconomic trends on the supply side of the supply-demand equation; relative changes in basic factors of production—labor, capital, and technology—which combine to make export- and import-competing items.

Sometimes referred to as the "competitiveness" approach, the structuralist understanding of the reasons behind America's deteriorating trade record has two broad parts. The first element concentrates on a long-standing decline in America's productivity growth compared to productivity improvements in the economies of our chief trade competitors. Because of (1) a slowdown in U.S. product/process technological innovation, and (2) comparative declines in the availability of, and increases in the cost of, capital to American businesses, the United States is now strained to support high-cost labor inputs and achieve productivity advances equal to those attained by foreign producers.

The second component of the structuralists' trade deficit etiology centers on how national resources, as factors of production, are managed by American government and private enterprise in comparison to the way in which their respective resources are handled by our trade rivals. Lacking (a) a coherent, outward looking public industrial policy and (b) corporate strategies responsive to rapidly evolving global competition, America's export- and import-competing industries are devoid of means for orchestrating production equal in effectiveness to those of our foreign trade opponents. When monetarists speak of the global competitiveness of the U.S. economy, they mean the *price* competitiveness of its goods and services in foreign and domestic markets. When the structuralists talk of competitiveness, they mean the comparative *ability* of American producers to acquire and mobilize the constituent elements of those same goods and services.

We start our account of the structuralist position on the causes of the U.S. trade imbalance with the notion of "productivity." The structuralists distinguish themselves from the monetarists by maintaining, as do analysts at the American Productivity Center, that "the real problem for U.S. manufacturers isn't currency values but lagging productivity."[70] Since the early 1970s, the pace of productivity gains throughout the industrialized world, including Western Europe and Japan, has slowed, but "the decline in the ability of U.S. enterprises to increase their output from a given input appears to have been more pronounced than elsewhere."[71] Defined as changes in the ratio of production output value to units of input compared to changes abroad, relative productivity is the structuralist key to the evolution of the American trade deficit.

As the reader may be aware, "productivity" does *not* refer to how hard, how well, or how efficiently the American workforce does its job. It is, however, conventionally qualified as "labor" productivity. Why this qualification? The input/output relationship upon which the productivity concept is based requires specification of which input(s) to which output(s) we are measuring in order to become operationally useful. Looking at output first, the obvious and customary definition is the value of that produced. This seemingly straightforward glossing has its own conceptual shortcomings. As Ira C. Magaziner and Robert B. Reich caution us, output assayed as the market or sales value of that produced does not capture new product modifications over time, especially product improvements that reduce real prices (sales values) of these goods.[72]

If the output aspect of productivity suffers from significant and unresolved conceptual problems, the input side is vulnerable to even more serious challenges. In the most simplified account, inputs include labor, capital, and technology, but there are difficulties in specifying each as units of input. How, for example, do we assess capital's contribution to each unit of output? Is it by simply aggregating fixed and variable production costs and then dividing them by the market value of associated output? Does it include the cost of acquiring capital in the form of interest payments or dividends to external creditors/investors? What of the cost of expending capital on the production of a particular unit as opposed to other production/investment opportunities foregone? And how in the world do we measure technology as a unit of output? Is it on the basis of research and development expenditures, the gains from plant modernization, or innovative changes in work procedures?

The customary (and wholly unsatisfactory) solution to this knot of problems is to adopt the method employed by the Department of Labor's Bureau of Labor Statistics. That is, to speak of labor productivity and treat capital and technology inputs as somehow being "neutral" constants. On this basis, national productivity, for example, is derived through dividing GNP or GDP by total worker hours of labor.[73] Acknowledging the conceptual and analytical defects of (labor) productivity calculated in this manner, unless otherwise specified, I am compelled to mean the ratio of units of output (current domestic market value) to worker hours of labor employed in their production when I refer to "productivity."

As the structuralists trace it, the United States has witnessed its own productivity growth lag behind those of its chief international competitors since the beginning of the 1960s. Table 4 provides a comparison of productivity increases in America's manufacturing sector with corresponding increases in productivity for Japan and Western European economies between 1960 and 1979. What we discover, in general, is that the United States trailed its principal trade rivals in productivity growth during the whole of the period in question and that our relative slowdown was greater in its latter half. According to another set of figures, output per worker hour of labor in all sectors of the American economy grew at a 2.6 percent annual rate between 1960 and 1978, while West Germany, France, and Japan turned in yearly gains of 5.5 pecent, 5.6 percent, and 8.5 percent respectively.[74] Between 1973 and 1979, Western European productivity grew at a rate twelve times that of the United States, while Japan enjoyed 14.5-fold faster productivity growth.[75] In the years from 1979 to 1984, America's annual percentage increases in labor

Table 4
Growth of Labor Productivity in Manufacturing for Six Nations, 1960–1979 (1960 = 100)

Year	United States	Japan	West Germany	United Kingdom	France	Italy
1960	100	100	100	100	100	100
1965	123	141	133	118	126	151
1970	141	258	174	142	178	188
1975	164	333	222	167	217	233
1979	185	445	280	180	282	290

Source: Yoshi Tsurumi, "Japan's Challenge to the United States: Industrial Policies and Corporate Strategies," Revitalizing American Industry: Lessons from Our Competitors, eds. MIlton Hochmuth and William Davidson (Cambridge, Massachusetts: Ballinger Press, 1985), p. 51.

productivity rose from an average 0.2 percent (1973 to 1979) to 0.7 percent, but still lagged behind Japan (2.6 percent) and the European Economic Community (1.5 percent).[76] Finally, between 1973 and 1984 as a whole, output per worker hour in the U.S. *manufacturing sector* grew at 2.0 percent a year, compared to 3.5 percent in West Germany, 4.5 percent in France and 6.7 percent in Japan.[77]

In the most recent periods for which such statistics are now available, U.S. productivity growth rates have undergone a deep low. In 1985, American nonfarm productivity actually *fell* some 0.2 percent, the first decline of this sort since the 1982 recession,[78] while productivity in all sectors of the economy (agriculture included) rose a mere 0.1 percent.[79] During the first quarter of 1986, nonfarm productivity improved to a 3.4 percent annualized rate of increase, but even with this spurt included, American productivity gains between 1982 and the first quarter of 1986 have averaged 1.3 percent on a yearly basis, far lower than in any corresponding post-World War II recovery period.[80] As to our chief trade competitor, Japan, its manufacturing productivity gains decreased dramatically in the 1973 to 1984 period when compared with the torrid pace they maintained between 1960 and 1973. However, owing largely to the speed with which the Japanese have put "new wave" automation into place in their manufacturing facilties, Japan's productivity growth has picked up steam in the mid-1980s.[81]

The dismal performance of the United States in its rate of productivity growth over the past twenty-five years, however, must be seen against the backdrop of the extraordinary productivity *levels* which the United States had achieved prior to this period. As Martin Baily and Alok Chakrabati relate, since the United States enjoyed the world's highest level of productivity by a wide margin in the past, "although not growing as rapidly, the level of productivity in the United States is as high or higher than that achieved overseas in most industries."[82] Many of their critics berate the structuralists for using productivity scare tactics and conveniently ignoring the fact that American productivity is, on the whole, among the highest in the world.[83] Indeed, when measured in terms of value added per work hour, America's manufacturing sector is still so ne 15 percent more productive than

Japan's.[84] Nevertheless, the positive productivity gap between the United States and its most advanced trade rival has been almost bridged. In certain industries (steel, autos, consumer electronics), especially those featuring multistep, high-volume assembly, Japanese productivity levels now surpass those of their American counterparts.[85] It is by no means a coincidence that it is in just these industries that American producers have ceded domestic and world market shares to Japanese manufacturers.

If America's productivity levels remain above, or, at least, equal to those of most of our international competitors, why is productivity identified as the underlying cause of the United States trade deficit by the structuralists? A large part of the answer lies in the fact that while the United States enjoys comparatively high production output per worker hour of input, the cost of hourly wages to American businesses has generally been much greater than that abroad. In other words, we are less competitive than others on this count because our industries suffer from a stiff labor cost disadvantage. Although wages are but one element of total production costs, when both direct and indirect labor costs are summed together, they are the largest such component. Moreover, owing to the fact that a nation's labor endowment is relatively fixed in comparison to internationally mobile capital and technology, there tends o be greater variation in average wage costs across countries compared to the relative uniformity of capital and technology costs.[86]

In calculating wage differentials between the United States and its foreign trade challengers, it must be remembered that, when stated in terms of dollars, these differentials are strongly influenced by the relative strength or weakness of the dollar. To illustrate this point, prior to September 1985 (when the dollar was seriously overvalued against the yen), the typical American factory worker earned 40 percent more than his Japanese counterpart in dollar figures, but, by August 1986 (as our currency had depreciated sharply against the yen), United States assembly-line workers earned about 12 percent less than comparable Japanese laborers in terms of dollars.[87] Thus we find that the structuralists cannot escape those basic macroeconomic conditions which function as the heart of the monetarist analysis in making their own assessment of the trade deficit's causes. However, in contrast to the monetarists, structuralists take wage differentials as the primary or substantive factor, relegating exchange rates to a secondary or modifying role. In addition, the structuralists note that when compared to wage rates in nations whose currencies have not appreciated against the dollar since early 1985, the gap between American labor costs and those abroad cannot be explained as a product of exchange rates.

In 1985, according to U.S. Bureau of Labor statistics, the average hourly compensation of American manufacturing sector workers was $12.82. From the standpoint of labor cost competitiveness, this rate compared disfavorably with similar hourly pay of $6.42 in Japan, $1.90 in Taiwan, $1.68 in Mexico, $1.32 in South Korea, and $1.30 in Brazil.[88] True, currency realignments in 1985 and 1986 caused Japanese labor costs to increase dramatically next to American rates, but in the case of the other countries mentioned, the same exchange rate–based narrowing of wage differentials has not occurred. Pay and benefits for Canadian auto workers remain some 30 percent lower than those in the American car industry;[89] South Korean auto workers receive about $2.16 an hour at present, and that nation's electronic consumer goods workers are paid an average $1 an hour;[90] American workers in California vineyards reportedly make $10 an hour in total compensation while Mexican grape pickers receive $2 to $3 a day.[91]

There is another facet of international wage differentials that figures prominently in the structuralist account of the U.S. trade deficit. Between 1975 and 1985, American manufacturing unit labor costs rose in dollar terms by about 50 percent compared with an increase of 25 percent in West Germany and a dollar-denominated decline of 10 percent in Japan.[92] This, of course, helps to explain the labor cost advantage of Japan and West Germany in the past, i.e., before the exchange rate changes of 1985 and 1986. But how does it contribute to our understanding of a growing bilateral trade deficit with these economies since the dollar's February 1985 peak? From the structuralist viewpoint, it was on the basis of lower labor factor costs that Japan and West Germany seized global and U.S. market shares from American industries. However, subsequent changes in these costs do not necessarily mean that U.S. producers can recoup market shares at home or abroad.[93] In those basic industries in which American wage rates were much higher than the national average—for example, steel and autos[94]—a labor factor advantage enabled Japan and Western European exporters to penetrate the U.S. domestic market (and compete successfully against American goods in third-country markets), gains which they can now sustain through other factors such as advanced production processes or perceived product quality. Indeed, part of the profits they have reaped by increasing their sales to the United States and the world have been used to finance those product/process improvements which allow our trade adversaries to keep market shares. What we discover, then, is that American manufacturers are presently disadvantaged by current wage differentials in some cases *and* by the residual effect of previous differentials in others.

There is a final aspect of labor's role in the decline of United States productivity competitiveness which is far more disturbing than the fact that American workers make (or did make) more in dollar terms than foreign workers. For more than two decades, the growth rate of skilled labor as a percentage of the total national workforce in the United States has been slower than abroad. For example, between 1963 and 1975, skilled labor's share of total American labor increased at an annual pace of 1.27 percent.[95] Over the same period, Brazilian, South Korean, Mexican, Japanese, British, French, and West German skilled labor grew as a proportion of their respective labor forces at rates of over 3.0 percent a year.[96] The relatively poor record of American increases in skilled labor means that our producers have been handicapped in (a) having a workforce whose overall skill levels are now being surpassed in foreign economies and (b) having to pay a wage premium to attract skilled workers.

These observations about the skill composition of the U.S. workforce lead us to briefly examine our educational system in (inevitable) comparison with Japan's. As reflected in educational attainments, the American populace displays a gaping "hole." On the one hand, approximately 60 percent of the U.S. college-age population cohort was enrolled in higher education in 1981, far higher than anywhere else.[97] On the other, it has been estimated that between 25 million and 30 million adult Americans cannot read and that another 35 million are functionally illiterate.[98] Approached from another angle, this same hole is demonstrated by the fact that 80 percent of all Americans complete high school, whereas in Japan the comparable figure is over 94 percent.[99] As the skill requirements of even the most basic manufacturing jobs increase with accelerating technological advances, a large portion of the U.S. workforce simply cannot fulfill them because they lack essential reading and math abilities.

But what of America's college-educated workers? The unvarnished truth lies in what has become something of a folk adage in the United States, to wit: What ails this country is a shortage of engineers and a surfeit of lawyers.[100] From a college population one-fifth the size of the United States, Japan graduates 75,000 engineers a year, some 3,000 more than America: Each year U.S. law schools churn out 612,000 attornies (two-thirds of the world's supply), while Japan graduates but 12,000.[101] All of this boils down to two points: (1) The overall skill composition of the American workforce has been declining relative to that of other nations; and (2) the most skilled segment of our workforce trails far behind Japanese and Western European counterparts in exactly those areas which contribute to international competitiveness, such as engineering, computer sciences, foreign language skills, etc. In short, American employers have been paying more for labor and receiving progressively less in terms of those skills which count in meeting the challenge of foreign production.

The second factor of production encompassed in the structuralist analysis of America's declining capacity to compete is capital. As Ira C. Magaziner and Robert B. Reich relate: "The most pervasive explanation of the slowdown in U.S. productivity growth, both absolute and relative, cites the decline in physical capital formation and the concomitant low level of capital expenditure compared to those of our major trading partners."[102] Since the early 1960s, America's share of total world capital has been shrinking.[103] Partially as a result of this erosion in America's former capital abundance, the percentage of our GDP devoted to capital formation has declined relative to the proportion of GDP dedicated to capital formation abroad. As the growth of capital expenditures by American businesses has lagged behind that of foreign producers, our own growth in capital per worker has necessarily fallen behind capital-to-worker ratio increases overseas. What all of this means is that American producers have not spent as much on plant/equipment modernization as foreign businesses. Operating older machinery and using a smaller percentage of state-of-the-art production processes, workers in the United States have been hamstrung in striving to increase their output at the same pace as foreign workers. Ergo, American productivity growth has lagged.

As with much of the structuralist argument, the deterioration in America's former capital factor cost advantage is a longstanding phenomenon, a trend which has been in force for over a quarter of a century. For instance, between 1961 and 1976, U.S. capital formation as a percentage of GDP averaged 17.8 a year. The corresponding figures for Canada, France, West Germany, and Japan were 22.2 percent, 23.2 percent, 24.3 percent, and 33.0 percent respectively.[104] Currently, new capital formation in Japan is some three times higher than in the United States.[105] Looking at capital spending by private enterprise, we find that West European corporations increased their capital outlays at an average of 3.0 percent a year between 1975 and 1985, while American companies raised their capital expenditures by a mere 0.7 percent per annum.[106] In 1981, the 1000 largest American manufacturing firms spent $102 billion in capital outlays. In 1983, however, these same companies spent but $76 billion, followed by $90 billion in 1984 and an estimated $101 billion in 1986.[107] The 1986 forecast now appears overly optimistic. In the fall of 1985, U.S. corporate executives surveyed by the Commerce Department reported that they planned to increase capital spending by 2.4 percent in 1986 over 1985 levels. By June 1986, planned expenditures for 1986 reported to the Commerce Department were cut back to 0.2 percent above 1985's totals.[108] Worse, in September of the same year, this poll found business spending plans for 1986 coming in at 2.5 percent *below* those of 1985.[109] In fact, during the first half of 1986, actual investment in plant and equipment by American business was 2.6 percent lower than in the corresponding period of 1985.[110].

With capital expenditures by American business lagging behind those of foreign companies, capital to worker ratios have followed a parallel course. Between 1963 and 1975, U.S. firms increased capital spending per worker at a rate of 1.7 percent a year. Over that time span, Korean companies raised capital spending per worker at a rate of 11.9 percent a year. Japanese, French, West German, and Canadian companies posted increases at rates of 10.1 percent, 5.8 percent, 4.2 percent, and 2.7 percent respectively, with both Canada and France surpassing the United States in capital stock per worker during this period.[111] In the following decade, while the United States increased its capital stock at a 2.0 percent annual pace, Japan's corresponding yearly rate was 6.0 percent, so that by 1979, Japanese capital equipment per worker reached the American level and now far exceeds it.[112] The result is that foreign productive facilities are now more capital intensive than plants in the United States. The impact of this is evident when we consider that our capital-intensive industries, e.g., steel, concurrently find themselves hard-pressed to compete against foreign goods in domestic and external markets.[113]

Probing the reasons behind this erosion in America's capital spending, we again discover an overlap between the structuralist and monetarist positions. Low (and declining) domestic savings rates combined with strong public/private demand for credit has put American firms at the disadvantage of facing a much higher cost of capital than foreign producers. This was not always the case. Until the early 1970s, the cost of capital in the United States was generally lower than in Japan and Western Europe, except when the governments of the latter provided subsidies to select corporate recipients. Since that time, however, the cost of capital in the economies of our trade competitors has been lower overall than in the United States.[114] For example, between 1975 and 1985, Japanese companies (assisted by their government's "guidance" of lending institutions) have been able to raise capital in domestic credit markets at a cost one-half that of American corporations.[115]

Beyond those broad, macroeconomic conditions that have contributed to comparatively high real interest rates on loans to American corporations, the structuralists point to differences in the way in which capital is normally raised by U.S. businesses compared to external financing patterns elsewhere. Japanese and West European enterprises typically maintain much closer relationships with their banks than American firms do with U.S. lending institutions. Foreign banks often have large equity stakes in the businesses they finance, creating a bank-client bond generally absent in the United States.[116] Moreover, foreign governments, most notably Japan's, actively encourage private bank lending to high-risk/high-growth ventures by permitting them to extend credit to companies with high debt-to-equity ratios. This contrasts with stringent American bank regulations which prohibit bank loans to companies having outstanding liabilities in excess of assets.[117] As a rule, both Japanese and Western European firms rely on banks and long-term bonds to a much greater extent than American companies that draw a greater portion of their external funding from fickle and high-cost stock markets.[118] Even in the case of equity issues, American corporations are disadvantaged by the fact that shareholders generally demand higher dividends than foreign investors.[119] Dependence upon the stock market for capital has had especially adverse consequences for small, technology-intensive American firms.[120] With these markets now dominated by risk-adverse institutional investors, small innovative outfits with the potential to become globally competitive have been spurned lately in favor of Blue Chip conglomerates, a point exemplified by the difficulty which American semiconductor manufacturers have had in acquiring equity funding.[121]

The third factor of production that has had a part in America's productivity slowdown is that of applied technology. At one point in time, American producers were able to offer workers generous pay scales and compensate for this labor cost disadvantage through technologically advanced products and production processes. Such is no longer true. While it is extraordinarily difficult to measure the contribution of technological innovation to increased productivity,[122] in "all studies of growth in advanced countries [it is] technological advance, not simply increases in numbers of machines or the amount of capital or labor [that] is at the core of sustained increases in productivity."[123] According to a study commissioned by the Japanese government, "technological development" was singled out as the most important force in Japan's industrial output growth,[124] while analogous research in the United States confirms that between 50 percent and 60 percent of American productivity increases are derived from "technological innovation."[125] Indeed, Martin Baily and Alok Chakrabati assert that the strongest factor retarding American productivity growth since the mid-1960s has been the marked slowdown in the nation's product/process innovation pace.[126]

Since determining just what constitutes a technological innovation is a slippery undertaking (to say nothing of aggregating and measuring the value of such innovations), structuralists have focused on two broad "clues" in contending that the United States has trailed behind its trade competitors on this front. The first clue is reflected in the levels, purposes and organizational modes of research and development in America compared to those abroad. The roughest index of relative R & D efforts by different nations is that of the percentage of GNP devoted to expenditures on research and development. According to Yoshi Tsurumi, total American expenditures on R & D peaked in 1964 at 2.9 percent of GNP and then declined progressively over the next fifteen years.[127] Simultaneously, Japan's GNP/R & D ratio rose from 1.2 percent in 1960 to 2.48 percent in 1980, surpassing the American ratio in that year.[128] Part of the slowdown in national R & D spending during this time was the result of cutbacks in government-funded research during the Vietnam era.[129] Nevertheless, as brought forth in recently published data, real (inflation-adjusted) R & D spending by American private enterprise dropped from an average annual 10.8 percent rate of increase in the period running from 1953 to 1963, to a mere 0.8 percent average yearly growth rate from 1963 through 1978.[130] It must be mentioned that in an effort to recover some of its lost technological edge, American corporate R & D spending has undergone a strong resurgence in the mid-1980s, posting growth rates of over 8 percent in 1984, 1985, and (est.) 1986.[131] This spurt, however, can be taken as the recognition by American corporations that past neglect of R & D has been a principal factor in the decline of their ability to compete on a global footing.

There is, moreover, a sharp divergence between the purposes to which the United States channels its research and development resources, on the one hand, and the objectives at which foreign R & D is aimed, on the other. In the United States, approximately 69 percent of annual national R & D expenditures come from the federal government. Of these, about one-half are devoted to military-related research, another 22 percent to aerospace projects.[132] In Japan, three-quarters of the country's yearly R & D outlays are expended by private firms, the remainder being nonmilitary spending by government, often in joint programs with industry.[133] Hence, while the bulk of America's R & D effort is given over to projects with little or no commercial value, the lion's share of Japan's research endeavors is "directly targeted at the commercialization of scientific and technical breakthroughs."[134] Indeed, if military research is excluded, Japan, with a GNP little more than one-half our own, is already devoting about as many man hours to research and development as the United States.[135]

The allocation of R & D resources to military versus commercial projects in the United States, as opposed to Japan, has a strong impact on the organizational modes through which research is conducted in the two nations. In Japan, most R & D occurs in state-of-the-art facilities *within* large manufacturing corporations. In the United States, since defense/space projects consume such a large portion of national R & D money and technological talent, commercially oriented research is performed mostly by small, innovative companies that sell their innovations to the highest bidders, including our foreign trade competitors.[136]

The second structuralist clue to the comparative decline of innovation in the United States is located in patent data trends. As Raymond Vernon comments, on the basis of national patent and international cross-patent applications/grants, America's relative technological slowdown appears "much greater than the concurrent decline in R & D expenditures."[137] In absolute terms, the number of patents issued to American inventors in the United States peaked in 1972 and declined steadily over the next ten years.[138] In 1972, the number of patent applications submitted in Japan surpassed those registered in the United States. Indeed, by 1978, as Japanese patents in their home country were two-thirds greater than in the United States, the number of patent applications from Japanese inventors to American authorities exceeded American patent submissions to Japanese officials.[139]

Overall, between 1961 and 1982, the fraction of the U.S. patents granted to foreign inventors rose from 16 percent to 41 percent.[140] Again, the diversion of America's research and development efforts to military and aerospace projects has had a major role in the relative decline of the country's former technological edge in products and manufacturing processes. Of the 30,000 patents owned by the federal government, less than 5 percent are licensed for commercial use.[141]

Critics of the structuralist argument on the relationship between America's innovational slowdown and its international competitiveness frequently assert that during the 1960s a "technological plateau" was reached worldwide insofar as manufacturing processes are concerned.[142] Hence, it follows that a technologically "mature" United States would experience a loss of relative innovational momentum, since its competitors had ample room to catch up on, while America had already come to a point of diminishing returns. The validity of this argument has been all but completely negated by the fact that the entire industrial world is now in the midst of a manufacturing revolution. Computer-aided design (CAD), computer-aided manufacturing (CAM), computer-integrated manufacturing (CIM), flexible manufacturing systems (FMS), robotics, etc., all spell a new generation of highly automated production processes which are currently being put into operation in the world's most advanced plants.[143] Slashing direct and indirect labor costs by two-thirds, permitting huge savings on materials and inventories, reducing break-even capacity points by one-half, adding "economies of scope" to economies of scale, these manufacturing innovations offer their users a host of competitive advantages and the opportunity to post overall productivity gains by giant leaps and bounds.[144]

Many of the technical breakthroughs upon which this new wave industrial revolution is based were originated in American laboratories.[145] However, while the United States remains ahead of its trade competitors in the invention of highly advanced production processes, it has fallen behind its chief commercial rival, Japan, in their actual application. In the United States, "only about two dozen companies have factories that even come close to the goal of total automation" with the "vast majority of U.S.

manufacturers sitting on the sidelines."[146] Although American engineers are still at the forefront in designing industrial robots, for example, presently Japan has as many industrial robots as the rest of the world combined and its introduction rate for these units is several times that of the United States.[147]

Part of the problem is money. Many American manufacturers have been either unable or unwilling to undertake the staggering commitment of capital necessary to upgrade their facilities to fully automated status. However, another factor that has contributed to America's lackluster showing on this count is an inadequate number of electrical engineers in its manufacturing sector. Putting automated systems in place requires detailed work by armies of electrical engineers, so that while America can outperform Japan in designing tomorrow's factories, our proportionate lack of engineering manpower has held us back from attaining a commensurate pace/level of application.[148]

To this juncture, we have looked at how differences in labor, capital, and applied technology between the United States and its main trade rivals have worked to its disadvantage. Along the way, it has been implied that all parties are basically producing the same output from those inputs. There is, nonetheless, a point at which the quantity of that produced must be distinguished from its perceived and objective *quality*. As previously mentioned, the structuralists argue that Japan and West European products initially took market shares from American wares on the basis of factor cost advantages which translated into relatively lower prices compared to those on our goods.[149] Once this cost-based penetration was accomplished, our competitors used past earnings and continued cost edges to enhance the quality of their products. Hence, Japanese and West European goods are no longer favored by American and foreign consumers on the grounds of cost alone, but also because they are seen by many as being of higher quality.[150] In large part, Americans buy Japanese products due to their reputation for reliability and West European items owing to their superior design, while for foreign consumers "made in America" is often taken as synonymous with "careless and shoddy."[151]

Such widespread perceptions are in themselves enough to account for the worsening of American bilateral trade balances with these nations, but, as anyone familiar with the ratings of *Consumer Reports* is aware, many Japanese and West European products do appear to be *better* than comparable American merchandise. Take, for instance, a ubiquitous item in the modern world, the random access memory (RAM) chip. In 1979, Hewlett-Packard tested failure rates for over 300,000 16K RAMS manufactured by three Japanese and three American suppliers. The outcome: the worst Japanese supplier's chips were six times more reliable than those from the best American producer.[152] More recently, in 1986, an American computer expert estimated that the typical yields of Japanese 256K RAMS were triple those of American chips.[153] Consequently, not only are foreign manufacturers getting more out of their factor inputs in quantitative terms, their factor cost advantages have been transmuted into superior products, allowing them to retain market shares even when their factor costs approach those of industry in the United States.

THE STRUCTURALIST POSITION: PART II

The other set of causes in the structuralist version of America's competitiveness slippage, and hence its trade deficit, concerns how different governments manage national resources and how corporate leaders in various countries respond to international competitive challenges. The most appropriate starting point for approaching the first of these matters is by examining a topic which we have already encountered under the monetarist rubric, that is, protectionist-mercantilist policies followed by our chief trade adversaries. To begin, although the structuralists concur with monetarists that *direct* foreign protectionism is *not* a major source of American trade imbalances, in the case of certain nations and particular sectors, tariff barriers have played a marginal role in generating our trade deficits. For example, Taiwan still maintains inordinately harsh import duties of between 40 percent and 50 percent on consumer goods (indeed, its government derives a full 20 percent of its revenues from tariff imposts).[154] It is, above all, in the agricultural sector that a strong case can be made for American exports being impeded by explicit tariffs. Taiwan and South Korea impose extraordinarily stiff levies on grain and meat imports. Japan allows some bulk agricultural commodities to enter its domestic market without crippling tariffs, but others, such as meat, oranges, and processed foods,[155] are heavily taxed to accommodate the nation's small, but politically powerful, farm lobby.[156] The same can be said of external tariffs on agricultural goods entering Western Europe under the weight of the E.E.C.'s blatantly protectionist Common Agricultural Policy (CAP).[157] In some instances, and especially where farm exports are involved, foreign tariff schedules have clearly hurt America's trade performance.

Since, however, Japanese, Canadian, and West European duties on manufactured goods are generally low, transparent tariff measures do not appear to have played a prime part in that sector which accounts for the brunt of the United States trade imbalance. The structuralist explanation is that it has generally been through the use of nontariff or intangible barriers that foreign government policies have inflicted harm upon American manufactured exports. With Japan serving as a model of how nontariff barriers (NTBs) have discouraged increased sales of American-made goods in overseas markets, three broad types of obstacles have been cited: (1) product standards and testing procedures; (2) government procurement policies; and (3) wholesale and retail distribution networks.[158]

Identified by Dorothy Christelow as the "most important intangible barrier"[159] to U.S. products competing in Japanese markets, product standards include: (a) minimum quality, health, and safety specifications required by various government agencies for all products sold in Japan; and (b) certifications of excellence for manufactured and agricultural goods which greatly enhance their saleability.[160] As to minimum standards, there is some direct evidence that American exports to Japan are subject to heavier burdens than domestically produced wares. For instance, the Japanese government refuses to accept foreign clinical data on the testing of new pharmaceutical products, meaning that U.S. drug exporters must incur the costs and delays of undergoing repeat testing under Japanese auspices.[161] Regarding "awards for excellence," the evidence of bias against foreign (U.S.) imports is less clear. Rigorous standards are applied to domestic and foreign products by, among others, the Japanese

Industrial Standards Committee, but it has been plausibly argued that on such discretionary points as product design, Japanese authorities naturally discriminate in favor of home-made items.[162]

Government procurement policies are an especially elusive species of NTB,[163] since subjective considerations freely mingle with such objective factors as speed of delivery when bureaucratic purchasing decisions are made. Nevertheless, Secretary of Commerce Malcolm Baldridge has complained that, while the American-made supercomputer Cray "is the standard by which the world builds super computers . . . we have yet to sell a single machine to a Japanese government bureau or to a Japanese university," and that the Japanese government "still refuses to allow government entities to purchase foreign satellites."[164] The zeal of Japanese civil servants in promoting their nation's interests, even when directed by elected superiors to "be fair," appears to have worked against the expansion of American exports to Japan.[165]

While Japanese government policies rankle American exporters, their experience with private distribution systems in Japan has been even more frustrating. Throughout East Asia, and most prominently in Japan, "indigenous distribution channels are thoroughly entrenched,"[166] supported by networks of group, family, and ethnic loyalties and a strong domestic orientation.[167] Distinguishing between domestic bias and objective forces keeping Japan's internal distribution system closed to foreigners is no easy task. In all good conscience, corporate purchasing agents, wholesalers, retailers, and the like can legitimately ask: Why should we take on foreign goods from outside suppliers having no track record in Japan when we already have well-established and extremely reliable ties with domestic sources?[168] Absent a prohibitively large discount on comparable items, foreign suppliers, including American exporters, have no truly satisfactory response to such rhetorical questions. More objectionable from the American exporter's point of view, Japanese intermediaries frequently tack on a surcharge to the imported goods they distribute. Average profit margins in Japan for retail sales of domestic liquor (23 percent), candy (27 percent), and cosmetics (33 to 40 percent) are much lower than those on imported liquor (70 percent), candy (54 to 60 percent), and cosmetics (65 to 90 percent).[169]

In evaluating the total impact of Japanese NTBs on American exports, the structuralists agree with the monetarists that, in the context of the huge U.S.–Japan trade imbalance, it is not large. In particular industries and product groups, e.g., agricultural goods, computers, drugs, and telecommunications equipment, American sales to Japan would increase substantially if all public and private intangible barriers were lifted.[170] Once again, however, a total increase of $5 billion to $7 billion in American exports to Japan would counterbalance but 10 percent to 15 percent of our bilateral trade deficit with the Japanese.

In fact, overt and clandestine import barriers by Japan and other major trading nations are an important part of a far larger structuralist concern, i.e., foreign industrial policies. With Japan as a central paradigm, the structuralists see comprehensive industrial policies directly interfacing with foreign trade performance. These policies tend to unfold in stages. In the first phase, after selecting target industries on the basis of their competitiveness potential, foreign governments nurture them by (1) providing protection in home markets against foreign competition and (2) granting them favorable treatment in the allocation of national resources, credit subsidies, for example. During the second stage, protection from foreign goods in domestic markets is decreased while affirmative treatment is continued or expanded. Hence, in a third and final period, having (1) achieved the benefits of scale economies and learning curve effects under a protectionist blanket and (2) bolstered productivity through the government-orchestrated channeling of capital, technology, and labor to them, these industries can compete at home and abroad without further government aid.

Examining the industrial policy scenario in closer detail, the structuralists assert that after World War II a new type of economy emerged in Europe and the Far East, one combining features of the free enterprise Anglo-American system with characteristics of the centrally planned structure of socialism.[171] In Japan and Europe, although market mechanisms continued to determine costs, prices, and "winners" from "losers," governments began to take an active role in fashioning their industrial

bases. At the start, the chief thrust came as protectionist regimes shielding rebuilt "infant industries" from foreign competition and nursing them to international competitive standards.[172]
Special treatment was reserved for industries with factor
advantages, perceived to have the potential to compete globally
once economies of scale were realized.[173] According to Clay
Woods, this first phase ended for Japan sometime in the mid-
1970s, but it continues in the case of others such as Taiwan,
South Korea, and Brazil, as evidenced in their maintenance of
flagrantly protectionist policies.[174]

In Japan, the second phase was reached as direct government
assistance to "sunrise" industries replaced protectionist devices. Earmarking certain sectors as internationally competitive,
the government, most especially through its Ministry of International Trade and Industry (MITI), actively promoted the most
outstanding firms within them, using initial export performance
as its central criterion in determining which companies deserved
assistance.[175] Beyond creating favorable macroeconomic envi-
ronments for these firms to work in (e.g., a savings-biased tax
regime), the Japanese government funneled public subsidies,
credit, and direct grants to targeted firms,[176] and used "admin-
istrative guidance" of the financial system to enhance this process. Indeed, in sharp relief to the U.S. Federal Reserve Bank,
the Bank of Japan took on an active, interventionist role in shap-
ing the course of national industrial development, literallly telling private banks where to invest their funds and to whom they
should extend low-cost credit.[177]

In the third, and present, stage of this process, the Japanese
government has shifted its focus from capital-intensive industries manufacturing standardized products to technology-intensive groups. This has been accompanied by a reduction in the
state's role as a source of capital assistance and a corresponding
expansion of its function in supervising national research and
development efforts. The government performs this orchestrating activity by encouraging and guiding firms within a given industry in pooling their resources and forming precompetitive
consortia with the participation of government and university
personnel.[178] These cooperative programs enable industries to
tackle research and development projects that individual firms

would otherwise find too costly or too risky to undertake by themselves. At this time, Japanese industrial consortia are working on nine so-called super projects, including the development of fifth-generation computers, optical technologies, and flexible manufacturing systems,[179] with MITI serving in an advisory/administrative capacity and private enterprise providing most of the capital and technical know-how.

Japan offers a model of industrial policy evolving in a highly deliberate and cohesive manner. When we turn to other American trade rivals, we find that their industrial policies are either less advanced and/or less methodical. Both South Korea and Taiwan have emulated the Japanese success story, adopting Japanese techniques to accelerate their national economic development. However, these Asian NICs still display features of "first phase" industrial policies, e.g., protection of infant industries, even as they move into more sophisticated functions such as the formation of technical consortia.[180] West European governments appear especially torn between old-style protectionism and the more innovative methods of industrial policy. On the one hand, both European agriculture and steel continue to receive direct financial asistance and import protection from the E.E.C. and its member nations. For example, under the E.E.C.'s Common Agricultural policy, some $21 billion a year in subsidies and price supports is paid to European farmers, accounting for 72 percent of the community's annual budget outlays.[181] Similarly, all of the major European powers extend import protection and financial aid to their respective steel industries.[182] In these cases, government intervention has been defensive and regressive in nature, propping up sectors/industries which would otherwise contract and which clearly lack the potential to upgrade their global competitiveness.

Simultaneously, the European community and individual West European states have begun to implement offensive and progressive industrial policy programs aimed at technologically advanced industries promising future international growth. France's Interministerial Committee for Strategic Industrial Development (CODIS) is now actively arranging precompetitive private R & D in twenty-three priority sectors (robotics, bio-tech, etc.), while the Federal Ministry of Research and Technology is performing a similar function in directing the development of West Germany's sunrise industries.[183] In addition, European governments are combining national resources in high-tech areas. The European Strategic Program for Research and Development in Information Technologies (ESPRIT), a five-year multinational program in the computer field, has generated a far more ambitious endeavor. Called "Eureka," this $1.9 billion research and development plan features participation by public and private organizations from eighteen countries in sixty-two separate projects, "aimed at developing everything from advanced software and new materials for automobiles to desert sunflower seeds and futuristic fishing boats."[184] Hence, although other U.S. commercial competitors do not boast the same step-by-step methodical approach to industrial policy as Japan, they have all initiated government action in spearheading drives to improve the global competitiveness of their economies.

Before examining the U.S. government's record in trade and industrial promotion, one final aspect of foreign government policies warrants consideration since it does have a decided impact upon America's trade performance. The policies in question are those which encourage or allow private foreign producers to pirate American-designed products. Affecting a wide range of items, but especially high-tech goods like computer software and drugs, this "nonpolicy" is most prevalent in the developing world, with Taiwan, South Korea, Brazil, and Mexico being prime examples. Defined as the unauthorized use of patents, trademarks, and copyrights (collectively termed "intellectual property"), it has been estimated that foreign piracy deprives rightful American owners of some $20 billion a year in lost sales and royalties by making/selling goods identical to American goods without permission, and even going so far as to attach bogus labels on them replicating the original producers' trademarks.[185] Some of these items are marketed abroad at deep discounts. It has been reported, for instance, that American-invented computer software having a list price of $500 in the United States is being sold in pirated form for $10 in the Far East.[186] A large portion of these items, moreover, makes its way to American markets since its entrance cannot be effectively monitored by an understaffed Customs Service.[187]

In the past, it was charged that the world's most prolific copy-cat was Japan, that "many Japanese products have basically been copies of foreign technology for which no recompense was made."[188] There are, however, two fundamental differences between Japan's penchant for imitating American-invented goods and the practices of modern pirates: (1) Japanese copies were not marketed as coming from original sources; (2) the Japanese government provides statutory protection against unadulterated piracy of intellectual property. In contrast, the Brazilian government offers no copyright protection for computer software, chemicals, or drugs; Malaysian penalties for copyright infringement are so light as to have no deterrent value; Indonesia has no patent law whatsoever. In essence, these governments have been committing sins of omission in turning a blind eye and a feeble hand to outright pilferage of American intellectual property by their citizens.

Returning to our central topic, the structuralist critique of the U.S. government's efforts to promote American global competitiveness includes both specific and general charges. In particular, the structuralists maintain that our government provides very little direct assistance to U.S. exports. Compared to programs abroad, the federal government's use of concessionary finance, loan guarantees, trade insurance, etc., to further export sales is extremely circumscribed.[189] Admittedly, through such agencies as the Export-Import Bank (EXIMBANK), the Commodity Credit Corporation (CCC), the Foreign Credit Insurance Association (FCIA) and the like, the U.S. government does extend marginal financial and technical assistance to American exporters.[190] When judged alongside their foreign counterparts, American export programs are drastically underfunded, restrictive in their product/market eligibility coverage, and generally neglectful of small- and medium-sized firms.[191]

This narrow bill of particulars has another side, one far worse from the structuralist standpoint. It has frequently been asserted that the U.S. government actually inflicts damage on America's trade performance through a range of export-control regulations. Approximately 30 percent of the country's manufactured exports (some one million separate items) cannot leave the United States without a government license because they are deemed

sensitive.[192] Other statutes prohibit export of certain national resources, oil from Alaska's North Slope and timber from federal
lands west of the 100th meridian, for instance.[193] Still others,
linked to political ends, bar shipment of a range of goods to
America's strategic foes, for example, grain and oil pipeline
equipment to the Soviet Union. The President's Commission on
Industrial Competitiveness has calculated that the federal government's export control laws result in $12 billion in lost Amer-
ican exports sales each year.[194] Private sources have estimated
that if Alaskan oil and federal timber were allowed to be delivered to Japan, one-half of our bilateral trade deficit with the Japanese would be eliminated.[195] Aside from lost sales, seemingly
arbitrary export control policies undermine the credibility of U.S.
suppliers in the eyes of foreign customers and deter joint enterprises with foreign companies.[196] Ironically, even in the case of
"national security" high-tech goods to the Eastern Bloc, these
controls have proven wholly ineffective. Faced with delays, un-
certainties, or outright proscriptions, foreign buyers simply turn
to alternative sources, i.e., our trade competitors, who are ready
and able to replace American goods.[197] What all of this amounts
to is that the U.S. government does little to help current and
potential American exports, while its export regulations do roughly
as much damage to America's trade balance as protectionist
measures on the part of our "unfair" trade rivals.

The other plank in the structuralist critique of the U.S. government's trade failures is far broader and anticipates the structuralists central policy prescription. Historically, the U.S. government has devoted scant attention to the external sector of the
American economy. Prior to the first oil shock, "the macroeconomic policy of the United States was almost exclusively formulated and conducted in terms of a closed economy."[198] Indeed,
as Penelope Hartland-Thunberg comments, it was not until the
Humphrey-Hawkins Act of 1978 that the country's balance-of-
payments position was mentioned as a national goal in a major
legislative bill.[199] The policy of successive administrations toward
the nation's international economic performance has consistently been one of counting on free market forces to correct temporary American setbacks in the long run.[200] While such laissez-
faire passivity may have been adequate in the past, as global

economic conditions have become more intensely competitive
and other nations have armed themselves with outward looking
industrial policies, the United States is shackled to "an out-
moded laissez faire philosophy unsuited to actual world conditions."[201] Our goverment has continued to place its faith in free
enterprise and broad macroeconomic policies as the answer to
any foreign trade problems, while our chief competitors have
supplemented macroeconomic management with comprehensive
structural strategies to improve their overall competitiveness in
the world.[202] Hence, Senator Danforth, noting that 1985 was the
tenth straight year of U.S. merchandise trade deficits, bitterly
complained of the Reagan administration's commitment to non-
intervention: "Passivity has been tried, and it doesn't work."[203]

The federal government's lack of commitment to international
trade is reflected in its organizational distribution of decision-
making power in the administration of policies which effect
America's trade performance. Almost without exception, our
foreign trade competitors have demonstrated firm support of their
export and import-competing industries by centralizing trade-related policy functions in a single, high-level body possessing
comprehensive authority, like Japan's MITI. Within the U.S.
government, there is no one agency or office charged with bolstering the nation's global competitiveness.[204] The Commerce
Department is the organizational unit within the federal government that handles the widest range of foreign trade duties. Despite the increased importance of foreign commerce to the
American economy, Commerce "is still organized as a service
bureau responsible for the census and weights & measures, and
not for an important policy-making role."[205] In the absence of a
central focus of trade/industrial competitiveness responsibility,
an inchoate assemblage of executive and legislative bodies for-
mulates and carries out this task. Given such fragmentation, the
U.S. government's industrial policy (if it can be called that) consists of ad hoc, piecemeal measures devoid of any overall strategy or direction.[206] Tax, anti-trust, occupational safety, and a
host of other policies all impact upon the ability of American
producers to meet the challenge of foreign competition, but they
are fashioned without apparent regard for it. Indeed, most of
these activities take the form of restrictions on business prac-

tices rather than affirmative supports. George Cabot Lodge has expressed the prohibitory nature of America's residual industrial policy in stating that "if the United States has had an explicit industrial policy in this century, it has been anti-trust."[207] The closest that any federal agency comes to positive support of private R & D on a significant scale, for instance, is the Pentagon's cooperative efforts with the arms and aerospace industries that have little value in terms of foreign trade. Thus, instead of an integrated set of trade- and competitiveness-related support programs governed by a unified body, America's industrial policy is comprised of haphazard policies executed through disparate agencies, many of them chartered to regulate businesses instead of assisting them.

The structuralists do not reserve all of their barbs for the public sector: Like the monetarists, they also find corporate America culpable in the worsening of the country's trade performance. Certainly the most prevalent charge against the private sector in the United States is its failure to develop a genuinely international perspective. Following World War II, American corporate management enjoyed decades during which it received praise from all corners of the world regarding its superior talents. A provincial arrogance was deeply embedded in our corporate culture based on the firm conviction that America's economic might would never be successfully challenged from abroad.[208] After all, not only did our producers possess seemingly unassailable advantages in capital and technology, they had unimpeded access to the world's largest and most vital domestic market. The sheer size of this homogenous outlet for their products virtually assured American manufacturers of stable and adequate demand for their wares, enabling them to standardize and automate production processes with the certain knowledge that these capital outlays would be matched by increasing sales revenues.[209] It was as a "bonus," that American business approached the export and direct investment opportunities available outside the United States, offering foreign consumers sophisticated products that their own plants could not yet manufacture. As foreign producers began to displace American-made items with the closing of the technology gap and the use of infant industry protectionism in the 1960s, this trend could be overlooked. American business would still have American markets to serve and all would remain right with the world.

Unfortunately, even as European and Japanese exporters began to make inroads into American markets, our corporate leaders considered such forays as anomalous departures from the norm, refusing to take cheap foreign imitations as a serious threat to their domestic hegemony. Moreover, they persisted in their insular preoccupation with internal consumption, relegating production for external markets to the bottom of their concerns. Rather than modify products and marketing strategies to fit local conditions abroad, they offered the world items fashioned according to American tastes and standards.[210] If foreign consumers did not rush to purchase these goods, this was interpreted as evidence of their backwardness and the need for time before they would share the same needs and wants as the American buying public.

In the interim, however, not only were foreign manufacturers finely attuned to the product requirements of their consumers, they began to look closer at the United States as well. In lieu of the "take it or leave it" attitude of American companies presenting domestic consumers with high-cost, energy-guzzling luxury items—after finding out what the mass of the American public really wanted—foreign corporations offered our consumers inexpensive, low-maintenance alternatives as Volkswagens began to appear alongside Impalas on American thoroughfares. In many instances, European and Japanese manufacturers effectively capitalized on advanced technological features invented by American engineers. Separating the "silver paper" from the "cheese," foreign producers took the truly worthwhile features of American products and incorporated them into superior designs.[211] Long after the need for a global viewpoint was apparent, American firms dismissed product/process innovations emanating from abroad, pretending that the United States was the sole source of such advancements. Hence, while our trade competitors were busily studying American markets and technical achievements, corporate management in the United States simply refused to widen its horizons.

Part and parcel with this narrow dismissal of global market and technological integration, America's corporate leadership

displayed a marked fixation with short-term profitability calculated through purely quantitative cost-benefit analyses. While our
trade rivals accorded top priority to long-term growth in market
shares, America's business strategists placed the maximization
of current net gains at the top of their agendas, being far more
anxious about quarterly dividends to shareholders than eventual
increases in sales volumes. Accustomed to four-decimal preci-
sion in making their cost-benefit decisions, American business
disregarded factors such as flexibility of production and product
reliability which could not be readily reduced to quantitative
terms.[212] Taking the highest possible return on investment as their
goal, and using stringent cost-benefit analysis as the basis for
attaining that end, American corporations focused on the luxury
end of the domestic market. Meanwhile, our trade competitors
adopted a far different tactic, concentrating on the lower, mass
end of the American market in which return on investment was
considerably lower. Harold Hall has succinctly outlined this alternative approach with specific reference to Japanese exporters:

By entering the low return segment of each industry, they encounter
little or no U.S. competition, but find spirited demand. Content with
their low rate of return, the Japanese rapidly gain share at the low end
of the market, and use the volume growth to fuel careful expansion up
the market.[213]

The same pattern is now developing in the cases of other American trade competitors, with, for example, South Korea aiming
its inexpensive Hyundai automobiles at the low end of the
American car market as a platform for following Japanese and
West European automakers into its higher brackets.

As the impact of their failure to compete against foreign imports mounted in the 1980s, America's corporate leaders tried to
adjust their production and marketing strategies. Although their
adjustment record is too short-lived to warrant any summary assessment of how well they are doing in response to the current
challenge, there are already some disconcerting signs on the ho-
rizon. In his study of the experience of West European firms
adjusting to low-cost foreign competition, Robert Grant's main

conclusion came in the form of serious doubts "as to the adequacy of cost reduction as a basis for the future competitiveness of U.S. industry."[214] Surveying corporate America's initial efforts to adjust to this same type of competition, Wickham Skinner observes that all too frequently American firms have chosen cost reduction methods as their chief means for boosting productivity.[215] Rather than upgrading facilities by making expenditures on technologically advanced production equipment, American manufacturers have often elected to simply cut back on costs. They have pared their capital outlays, and, in Skinner's opinion, this has had the effect of stifling innovation and undermining morale.[216] Instead of gearing up to meet the competition head on, many American companies have adopted a defensive "holding pattern" posture, seemingly unsure of their own ability to compete aggressively in a dynamic environment.

Since February 1985, the decline of the dollar against the yen and the Deutsche mark has presented American producers with the opportunity to regain domestic and external market shares from the Japanese and West Germans. Such tentative evidence as is now available indicates that many U.S. firms are simply not capitalizing on this opportunity. Rather than lower export prices in line with the dollar's decline, "some U.S. exporters are aiming for bigger profit margins by maintaining or even increasing prices."[217] The same can be said of our import-competing companies. Currency realignments have compelled some foreign producers to raise their prices on goods offered to American consumers, but rather than taking advantage of this chance to recoup lost domestic sales, all too many American manufacturers have hiked their prices as well, opting for fattened profit margins in the short run over long-term growth in sales volumes.[218]   The last facet of corporate America's role in its own competitive demise is one that previously received widespread attention, but that has now been subordinated to more pressing matters in the structuralist version of America's eroding competitiveness. In the late 1970s and early 1980s, a wave of books and articles appeared in the West extolling the virtues of Japanese management practices, particularly the harmonious character of labor-management relations in Japan.[219] Presented in pointed relief to the antagonistic nature of labor-management interaction in the United States, these studies spoke glowingly of the common bonds linking Japanese managers and workers. Offering lifetime employment, promotion from within, and a participatory, consensual approach to decision-making, Japanese managerial paternalism fostered loyalty and a commitment to quality on the part of subordinates.[220]

The unlimited enthusiasm of some Japan watchers may have been overly idealistic, but, without dwelling on the topic, there appears to be some element of truth in the claim that Japanese management style lends a competitive edge to their operations. To cite one telling anecdote, in 1984 the Japanese automaker Toyota entered into a joint program with General Motors to manufacture Chevrolet Novas. Japanese managerial personnel were assigned the task of overseeing operations at GM's Fremont, California plant. Although this facility suffered from out-of-date production equipment, its productivity remains higher than most of GM's new factories. "The key," we are told in the pages of a popular business journal, "is Toyota's management style, which emphasizes thorough training and participative management, lean layers of middle management and decision-making pushed as close as possible to the assembly line."[221] While tales like this one do not verify the claim that the Japanese generate productivity gains through superior management style, the higher reliability of their products and their lower employee turnover and absentee rates do suggest that Japanese management is doing something far better than its American counterpart.

CONCLUSION

Although the respective arguments of the monetarists and structuralists about the origins of America's worsening trade performance are not complete antitheses, it is hard to imagine two more divergent viewpoints on the topic. The two positions rest on vastly different assumptions about the relative importance of monetary versus real factors as causal agents contributing to the U.S. trade deficit. Consequently, there is simply no means of reconciling these alternative analyses. There are, however, two broad points which can be made about them without

endorsing either. First, as I have hopefully brought forth, both
versions offer us valuable insights into the sources of the American trade imbalance. Second, the two sides share a common
theme: The trade deficit is essentially the outcome of factors,
trends, and policies originating within the United States—not the
evil machinations of our trade competitors. As we proceed to
examine the meanings of the trade deficit from each of these
viewpoints in Chapter 3, another broad point of concurrence will
come to the fore: From their distinct vantage points, monetarism
and structuralism see the trade deficit as having profound consequences for the United States which may prove of lasting significance.

NOTES

1. Richard N. Cooper, "Dealing with the Trade Deficit in a Floating Rate System," *Brookings Papers on Economic Activity*, no. 1 (1986),
p. 202.

2. Paula Stern, "The U.S. Trade System and the National Interest," *Vital Speeches,* vol. lii, no. 13 (April 15, 1986), p. 390.

3. Ibid.

4. Vincent Reinhart, "Macroeconomic Influence on the U.S.–Japan Trade Imbalance," *Federal Reserve Bank of New York*, vol. xi,
no. 1 (Spring 1986), p. 6.

5. *New York Times*, May 4, 1986, p. F-10.

6. Robert V. Roosa, "The Gap between Trade Theory and Capital
Flows," *Challenge*, vol. xxvi, no. 1 (March–April 1983), p. 55.

7. Joint Committee of the Council of Economic Advisors, *Economic Indicators*, June 1986, p. 30.

8. Lawrence Minard, "Noah's Ark, Anyone?" *Forbes*, vol. cxxxvi,
no. 4 (August 12, 1985), p. 78.

9. Organization for Economic Cooperation and Development, *Financial Market Trends*, no. 34 (June 1986), pp. 97–98.

10. Vito Tanzi, "Fiscal Deficits and Interest Rates in United States:
An Empirical Analysis, 1960–84," *IMF Staff Papers*, vol. xxxii, no. 4
(December 1985), p. 572.

11. Allan H. Meltzer, "How to Cut the Trade Deficit," *Fortune*, vol.
cxii, no. 12 (November 25, 1985), p. 180.

12. Norman Gall, "Hold the Champagne," *Forbes*, vol. cxxxvii, no.
10 (May 5, 1986), p. 42.

13. C. Fred Bergstein, "The U.S.–Japan Trade Imbroglio," *Challenge*, vol. xxviii, no. 3 (July–August 1985), p. 17.

14. Tanzi, p. 571.

15. Cooper, pp. 73, 75.

16. Irwin L. Kellner, "Crowding Out," *Bankers Monthly*, vol. cii, no. 10 (October 15, 1985), p. 7.

17. Gall, p. 42.

18. *New York Times*, July 29, 1986, p. A-1.

19. Duane R. Kullberg, "The Deficit Is Worse Than It Looks," *Fortune*, vol. cxiii, no. 10 (May 12, 1986), p. 141.

20. Michael H. Hutchinson and Adrian W. Throop, "U.S. Budget Deficit and the Real Value of the Dollar," *Federal Reserve Bank of San Francisco Economic Review*, no. 4 (Fall 1985), p. 40.

21. Cooper, p. 198.

22. Henry Eason, "Keeping the Trade Deficit in the Right Perspective," *Nation's Business*, vol. lxxii, no. 10 (October 1984), p. 54.

23. *New York Times*, July 29, 1986, p. D-6.

24. Ibid.

25. Rachel McCulloch, "Point of View: Trade Deficits, Industrial Competitiveness and the Japanese," *California Management Review*, vol. xxvii, no. 2 (Winter 1985), p. 146.

26. Raymond Vernon, "The Analytical Challenge," *Revitalizing American Industry: Lessons from Our Competitors*, ed. Milton Hochmuth and William Davidson (Cambridge, Mass: Ballinger Press, 1985), p. 30.

27. Minard, p. 80.

28. Basil Caplan, "No Easy Solution to the Japan Trade Problem," *The Banker*, vol. cxxv, no. 715 (September 1985), p. 57.

29. Andrew Tanzer, "The Trouble with Mercantilism," *Forbes*, vol. cxxxviii, no. 3 (August 11, 1986), p. 42.

30. John D. A. Cuddy, "Some Reflections on Growth in OECD Economies," *Trade and Development*, no. 6 (1985), pp. 73–74.

31. George Marotta, "Our Domestic and International Deficits," *Vital Speeches*, vol. lii, no. 8 (February 1, 1986), p. 235.

32. Ira C. Magaziner and Robert B. Reich, *Minding America's Business: The Decline and Rise of the American Economy* (New York: Random House, 1983) p. 42.

33. Norma Gall, "A Yen to Spend," *Forbes*, vol. cxxxvii, no. 11 (May 19, 1986), p. 55.

34. Amitai Etzioni, *An Immodest Agenda: Rebuilding America before the Twenty-first Century* (New York: McGraw-Hill, 1983), p. 315.

35. *New York Times*, April 29, 1986, p. D-5.

36. Karel Van Wolferen, "The Japanese Economy," *Survey*, vol. xxix, no. 1 (Spring 1985), p. 178.

37. Bruce R. Scott, "Can Industry Survive the Welfare State?" *Harvard Business Review*, vol. lx, no. 5 (September–October 1982), p. 73.

38. Gall, "A Yen to Spend," p. 57.

39. Scott, p. 74.

40. "President Reagan Issues New Trade Policy," *Business America*, vol. viii, no. 20 (September 30, 1985), p. 7.

41. W. Allen Wallis, "Protecting Prosperity from Protectionism," *Department of State Bulletin*, vol. lxxxvi, no. 2108 (March 1986), p. 34.

42. Jeffrey H. Bergstrand, "United States–Japanese Trade Predictions Using Selected Economic Models," *New England Economic Review* (May/June 1986), p. 29.

43. Reinhart, p. 6.

44. Preston Martin, "Statement . . . before the Subcommittee on Economic Stabilization of the Committee on Banking, Finance and Urban Affairs, U.S. House of Representatives, July 18, 1985," *Federal Reserve Bulletin*, vol. lxxi, no. 9 (September 1985), p. 698.

45. Robin R. Marshall, "Japan and Germany: Recovery with Policy Stability," *The Banker*, vol. cxxxv, no. 707 (January 1985), p. 55.

46. Martin, p. 698.

47. Malcolm Baldrige, "Secretary Baldrige Urges Japan to Lower Trade Barriers," *Business America*, vol. ix, no. 16 (August 4, 1986), p. 3.

48. Reinhart, p. 9.

49. *New York Times*, October 8, 1986, p. D-2.

50. George Cabot Lodge and William C. Crom, "U.S. Competitiveness: The Policy Tangle," *Harvard Business Review*, vol. lxiii, no. 1 (January–February 1985), p. 41.

51. Scott, pp. 76–77.

52. Hannay and Steele, p. 20.

53. *New York Times*, August 24, 1986, p. F-2.

54. Lodge and Crom, p. 38.

55. Magaziner and Reich, p. 41.

56. Hannay and Steele, p. 18.

57. Baldrige, p. 5.

58. *Economist*, April 5, 1986, p. 77.

59. Dorothy Christelow, "Japan's Intangible Barriers to Trade in Manufactures," *Federal Reserve Bank of New York Quarterly Review*, vol. x, no. 4 (Winter 1985–86), p. 12.

60. Clay Woods, "The U.S. Computer Trade Surplus Erodes," *Business America*, vol. viii, no. 20 (September 30, 1985), p. 11.

61. Lee Smith, "What the U.S. Can Sell Japan," *Fortune*, vol. cxi, no. 10 (May 13, 1985), p. 93.

62. Ezra F. Vogel, "Pax Nipponica" *Foreign Affairs*, vol. 1765.

63. Christelow, p. 18.

64. Bergstrand, p. 26.

65. McCulloch, p. 155.

66. Norman S. Fiekle, "Dollar Appreciation and U.S. Import Prices," *Federal Reserve Bank of Boston: New England Economic Review* (November–December 1985), pp. 51–52.

67. Ibid., p. 54.

68. Robert Z. Lawrence and Robert E. Litan, "Living with the Trade Deficit: Adjustment Strategies to Preserve Free Trade," *The Brookings Review*, vol. iv, no. 1 (Fall 1985), p. 3.

69. *Businessweek*, June 23, 1986, p. 28.

70. Aloysius Ehrbar, "The Super Yen Won't Save the Day," *Fortune*, vol. cxiii, no. 3 (February 3, 1986), p. 73.

71. Vernon, pp. 25–26.

72. Magaziner and Reich, p. 55.

73. Thibaut de Saint Phalle, *Trade, Inflation and the Dollar* (New York: Oxford University Press, 1981), p. 286.

74. Jack Carlson and Hugh Graham, "The Economic Importance of Exports to the United States," *The Export Performance of the United States: Political, Strategic and Economic Implications*, ed. Jennifer J. White (New York: Praeger, 1981), pp. 125–26.

75. Cuddy, p. 49.

76. Ibid., p. 50.

77. Martin Neil Baily and Alok K. Chakrabati, "Innovation and U.S. Competitiveness," *The Brookings Review*, vol. iv, no. 1 (Fall 1985), p. 14.

78. *Dun's Business Month* (April 1986), p. 16.

79. *New York Times*, July 29, 1986, p. A-1.

80. *Businessweek*, May 12, 1986, p. 18.

81. Vogel, p. 753.

82. Baily and Chakrabati, p. 14.

83. Wallis, p. 33.

84. Inoguchi Takashi, "Japan's Images and Options: Not a Challenger, but a Supporter," *The Journal of Japanese Studies*, vol. xii, no. 1 (Winter 1986), p. 99.

85. James C. Abegglen and George Stalk, "The Japanese Corpora-

tion as Competitor," *California Management Review*, vol. xxviii, no. 3 (Spring 1986), p. 27.

86. Grant, p. 83.

87. *Businessweek*, August 18, 1986, p. 14.

88. Cited in Jackie Preser, "How to Stop Exporting U.S. Jobs," *Fortune*, vol. cxii, no. 7 (September 30, 1985), p. 105.

89. Edwin A. Finn and Richard C. Morris, "Good Neighbors Again," *Forbes*, vol. cxxxvii, no. 11 (May 19, 1986), p. 134.

90. Bruce Stokes, "Korea: Relations Worsen," *National Journal*, vol. xviii, no. 18 (April 5, 1986), pp. 814, 815.

91. *New York Times*, August 3, 1986, p. F-3.

92. *Businessweek*, May 12, 1986, p. 18.

93. Abegglen and Stalk, p. 22.

94. Milton Hochmuth, "Analysis and Summary," *Revitalizing American Industry: Lessons from Our Competitors*, ed. Milton Hochmuth and William Davidson (Cambridge, Mass.: Ballinger Press, 1985), p. 383.

95. Harry P. Bowen, "Changes in the International Distribution of Resources and Their Impact on U.S. Comparative Advantage," *Review of Economics and Statistics*, vol. lxv, no. 3 (August 1983), p. 404.

96. Ibid.

97. Robert C. Puth, "Human Mobility as a Source of American Economic Growth," *The Quarterly Review of Economics and Business*, vol. xxvi. no. 1 (Spring 1986), p. 70.

98. Herbert E. Striner, *Regaining the Lead: Policies for Economic Growth* (New York: Praeger, 1984), p. 130.

99. Vogel, p. 762.

100. Hannay and Steele, p. 22.

101. Robert McCurry, "Competing with Japan: Will the U.S. Seize the Opportunity?" *Vital Speeches*, vol. lii, no. 19 (July 15, 1986), p. 595.

102. Magaziner and Reich, p. 45.

103. Bowen, p. 405.

104. Magaziner and Reich, p. 45.

105. Harold H. Hall, "To Compete We Need Capital Accumulation," *Research Management*, vol. xxix, no. 3 (May–June 1986), p. 6.

106. David Fairlamb, "Europe Struggles to Catch Up," *Dun's Business Month*, vol. cxxv (April 1985), p. 72.

107. *New York Times*, August 12, 1986, p. D-1.

108. *New York Times*, August 25, 1986, p. D-7.

109. *New York Times*, September 12, 1986, p. D-1.

110. *New York Times*, July 23, 1986, p. D-13.

111. Bowen, p. 403.

112. *Businessweek*, May 12, 1986, p. 18.
113. Bowen, pp. 407–408.
114. Hochmuth, "Analysis and Summary", pp. 380–81.
115. Hall, p. 6.
116. Tsurumi, p. 64.
117. Etzioni, p. 314.
118. Ibid.
119. *New York Times*, August 13, 1986, p. F-4.
120. De Saint Phalle, pp. 305–306.
121. *Businessweek*, August 18, 1986, p. 63.
122. Vernon, p. 23.
123. Stephen S. Cohen and John Zysman, "Can America Compete?" *Challenge*, vol. xxix, no. 2 (May–June 1986), p. 62.
124. Tsurumi, pp. 50-51.
125. De Saint Phalle, p. 295.
126. Baily and Chakrabati, p. 630.
127. Tsurumi, pp. 52–53.
128. Ibid., p. 53.
129. Robert Z. Lawrence, "The Myth of U.S. Deindustrialization," *Challenge*, vol. xxvi, no. 5 (November–December 1983), p. 18.
130. *Businessweek*, June 16, 1986, p. 24.
131. Ibid.
132. Tsurumi, p. 53.
133. Ibid.
134. Ibid.
135. Vogel, p. 754.
136. Ibid.
137. Vernon, pp. 24–25.
138. Baily and Chakrabati, p. 15.
139. Tsurumi, pp. 54–55.
140. Baily and Chakrabati, p. 14.
141. E. Jonathan Soderstrom and Bruce M. Winchell, "Patent Policy Changes Stimulating Commercial Application of Federal R & D," *Research Management*, vol. xxix, no. 3 (May–June 1986), p. 35.
142. Martin Neil Baily and Alok K. Chakrabati, "Innovation and Productivity in U.S. Industry," *Brookings Papers on Economic Activity*, no. 2 (1985), p. 630.
143. Cohen and Zysman, p. 58.
144. *Businessweek*, June 16, 1986, pp. 100–101.
145. *Nation's Business* (February 1986), p. 65.
146. *Businessweek*, March 3, 1986, p. 74.
147. Vogel, "Pax Nipponica," p. 752.

84   U.S. Trade Deficit of the 1980s

148. Ibid, p. 753.
149. Hochmuth, "Analysis and Summary," p. 378.
150. Magaziner and Reich, p. 51.
151. Phyllis Birnbaum, "Honorable Fussy Customers," *Across the Board*, vol. xxiii, no. 3 (March 1986), p. 27.
152. Tsurumi, p. 69.
153. *Businessweek*, August 18, 1986, p. 63.
154. Tanzer, p. 42.
155. Donna V. Vogt, "Japanese Import Barriers to U.S. Agricultural Exports," *Congressional Research Service Review*, vol. vii, no. 2 (February 1986), p. 24.
156. Dick Wilson, "Japan: The Trade Challenge," *The Banker*, vol. cxxxii, no. 675, p. 31.
157. Joan Pearce, "Europrotectionism: The Challenge and the Cost," *The World Today*, vol. xli, no. 12 (December 1985), p. 227.
158. Christelow, p. 11.
159. Ibid., p. 12.
160. Ibid.
161. Smith, p. 95.
162. Vogel, "Pax Nipponica?" p. 760.
163. N. T. Wang, "Penetrating New Markets," *Academy of Political Science of New York City Proceedings*, vol. xxxvi, no. 1 (1986), p. 163.
164. Baldridge, p. 4.
165. Birnbaum, p. 26.
166. Wang, p. 164.
167. Wilson, pp. 31–32.
168. Joseph T. Enright, "Selling Consumer Goods in Japan," *Business America*, vol. ix, no. 5 (March 3, 1986), p. 3.   169. Birnbaum, p. 26.
170. Christelow, p. 16.
171. Herbert E. Striner, *Regaining the Lead: Policies for Economic Growth* (New York: Praeger, 1984), p. 34.
172. Vogel "Pax Nipponica?" p. 760.
173. Paul Krugman, "New Theories of Trade Among Industrial Countries," *The American Economic Review*, vol. lxxiii, no. 2 (May 1983), pp. 344–45.
174. Woods, p. 11.
175. Tsurumi, pp. 44–45.
176. Schultze, p. 6.
177. *New York Times*, June 9, 1986, p. D-4.
178. Herbert J. Fusfeld and Carmela S. Haklisch, "Cooperative R &

D for Competitors," *Harvard Business Review*, vol. lxiii, no. 6 (November–December 1985), p. 61.

179. Masaaki Kotabe, "Changing Roles of the Sogo Shoshas, the Manufacturing Firms and the MITI in the Context of the Japanese 'Trade or Die' Mentality," *Columbia Journal of World Business*, vol. xix, no. 3 (Fall 1984), p. 40.

180. Bruce Cummings, "South Korea: Trouble Ahead," *Current History*, vol. lxxxv, no. 510 (April 1986), p. 161.

181. *New York Times*, August 4, 1986, p. D-1.

182. Stefan A. Musto, "The Loss of Hegemony: Sensitive Industries and Industrial Policies in the European Community," *Europe at the Crossroads: Agenda of the Crisis*, ed. Stefan A. Musto and Carl F. Pinkele (New York: Praeger, 1985), p. 91.

183. David A. Heenan, "Building Industrial Cooperation Through Japanese Strategies," *Business Horizons*, vol. xxviii, no. 6 (November–December 1985), p. 11.

184. *New York Times*, July 1, 1986, p. D-11.

185. Eileen Hill, "The Administration Is Working to Improve World-Wide Protection of One of Our Most Valuable Assets: Intellectual Property," *Business America*, vol. ix, no. 15 (July 21, 1986), p. 9.

186. Ibid.

187. Bruce Stokes, "Intellectual Piracy Captures the Attention of the President and Congress," *National Journal*, vol. xviii, no. 8 (February 22, 1986), p. 444.

188. Ezra F. Vogel, "Dear America/Dear Japan," *Society*, vol. lii, no. 4 (May–June 1986), p. 48.

189. Wang, p. 165.

190. Hill, p. 8.

191. Hannay and Steele, p. 20.

192. *New York Times*, May 14, 1986, p. D-18.

193. Murray L. Weidenbaum, "Japan Bashing and Foreign Trade," *Society*, vol. xxiii, no. 4 (May–June 1986), p. 45.

194. *New York Times*, June 18, 1986, p. D-2.

195. Weidenbaum, p. 45.

196. Lodge and Crom, pp. 36–37.

197. Murray L. Weidenbaum, "Freeing Trade," *Beyond the Status Quo: Policy Proposals for America*, ed. David Boaz and Edward H. Crane (Washington: Cato Institute, 1985), p. 101.

198. M. A. Akhtar, "Policy Options in the U.S.," *Harvard International Review*, vol. viii, no. 1 (November 1985), p. 12.

199. Penelope Hartland-Thunberg, "The Political and Strategic Importance of Exports," *The Export Performance of the United States:*

Political, Strategic and Economic Implications, ed. Jennifer J. White (New York: Praeger, 1981), p. 32.

200. Striner, p. 34.

201. McCulloch, P. 143.

202. William E. Hudson, "The Feasibility of a Comprehensive U.S. Industrial Policy," *Political Science Quarterly*, vol. c, no. 3 (Fall 1985), p. 463.

203. Minard, p. 80.

204. Magaziner and Reich, p. 258.

205. Scott, p. 81.

206. Hudson, p. 465.

207. Lodge, p. 24.

208. Vernon, p. 31.

209. Carson and Graham, p. 128.

210. Vernon, pp. 33–34.

211. *Economist*, April 26, 1986, p. 19.

212. *Businessweek*, March 3, 1986, p. 74.

213. Hall, p. 6.

214. Grant, p. 95.

215. Wickham Skinner, "The Productivity Paradox," *Harvard Business Review*, vol. lxiv, no. 4 (July–August 1986), p. 55.

216. Ibid., pp. 56–57.

217. *Nation's Business*, September 1986, p. 10.

218. *Economist*, March 1, 1986, p. 59.

219. Hochmuth, "Analysis and Summary," p. 393.

220. Janet P. Near and Richard W. Olshansky, "Japan's Success: Luck or Skill?" *Business Horizons*, vol. xxviii, no. 6 (November–December 1985), pp. 16–19.

221. *Businessweek*, June 16, 1986, p. 104.

3

THE MEANINGS OF THE TRADE DEFICIT

THE MONETARIST POSITION

Although they are greatly outweighed by its negative consequences, the monetarist position does recognize a handful of
positive developments arising from the American trade imbalance and the inflow of foreign capital underwriting it. During the
first half of the 1980s, as other free-market economies were lan-
guishing in the aftermaths of energy shocks and foreign debt
overloads, by absorbing exports from them, the U.S. economy
functioned as an engine of growth, without which the world would
have undergone a far deeper and far longer recession. The strong
dollar, moreover, gave American consumers an import bargain,
and, with it, lower domestic price inflation than would otherwise
have been the case. The in-migration of foreign money into U.S.
investments permitted a higher level of capital formation than
that which could have been attained had America relied solely
on its own national savings. It also mitigated the crowding out
effect of federal government debt issues upon our credit markets, thereby keeping interest rates from rising. Unfortunately,
all of these benefits are either over or rapidly nearing their end.
Indeed, they can be seen collectively as a palliative which enabled America to temporarily avoid the pain of adjustment, just
as a narcotic allows a gravely ailing man to delay entering the
hospital. The nation's day of reckoning may have been pushed

forward through the impetus of foreign goods and money, but the longer it is put off, the larger and more ominous that day becomes.

The cardinal meaning of the U.S. trade deficit for the monetarists is that of a severe balance-of-payments problem with strong and diverse effects upon our economy. The accumulation of successive current account deficits occasioned by our perennial trade gaps has moved the United States into the position of being a net international debtor. For some time to come, America must relinquish a significant portion of the value of its national output to foreigners in the form of debt-service payments. Our capacity to generate the earnings/savings necessary to meet these external obligations is undercut by current and prospective trade imbalances. Since all of this occurs in a competitive context, the transfer of resources abroad eliminates their potential part in upgrading our competitiveness and augments the capacity of our trade rivals to improve theirs. The bottom line on this count, then, is that economic growth in the United States must slow substantially as we pay the price for overrapid expansion in the past, and, in fact, this slowdown is already taking place.

The policies adopted by the Federal Reserve Board will have a determining role in whether the American growth slowdown will assume the form of an abrupt plunge or a prolonged downtrend. Through its influence over domestic interest rates, the Fed can make U.S. investments less attractive to foreign savers, curbing debt-creating, import-financing capital inflows. Through its indirect influence on exchange rate movements, the Fed can take the same course, weakening the dollar to improve the price competitiveness of American goods and to deter foreign acquisition of dollar-denominated assets. These remedies, however, carry the seeds of their own negation. Driving down interest rates through expansionary monetary policies will ultimately reheat the American economy, causing an inflation-induced upward spike in domestic interest rates and the reproduction of those investment differentials that prompt foreigners to send their excess savings to the United States. Currency depreciation also carries an inflationary undertow, most directly in the form of raised prices on essential imports and production inputs, again exerting upward pressure on domestic interest rates. Economic stagnation periodically leavened by inflation-provoking monetary stimulation brings us back to a syndrome prevalent in the 1970s: the phenomenon of stagflation. From the monetarist viewpoint, this is the lasting legacy of the trade imbalances posted by the United States in the 1980s, and it is a cheerless one to say the least. Even this type of malaise, however, can be aggravated further through the impact of another outcome of our worsening trade performance, the chorus of cries for the adoption of protectionist measures to deal with it. Should our government appease the political interests behind the current protectionist clamor, both the economy in general, and its external sector in particular, will atrophy; hence, our ability to recover from balance-of-payments infirmity will progressively vanish.

Overlooked by most critics of America's eroding trade performance and greatly overemphasized in the trade deficit apologetics of the federal government, the bright side of the U.S. trade balance does have a part in the monetarist version of its meanings. The enormous expansion of imports into the United States in the first half of the 1980s provided our trading partners with a strong growth stimulus at a time when it was sorely needed. By vastly enlarging its role as an export outlet, America was virtually the only economy in the world keeping global trade afloat. This engine of growth function gave an especially welcome boost to the economies of Western Europe and, above all, the Third World. Regarding the former, the second OPEC oil shock sent European industry into a tailspin, its energy-intensive sectors reeling from the doubling of international petroleum prices between 1979 and 1982. Morbidly fearful of the erosive effects of domestic price inflation, West European fiscal and monetary authorities refused to use expansionary measures to lift growth rates in their economies. Consequently, Europe stagnated in the early 1980s, with GNP growth averaging a mere 2 percent or less a year and unemployment rates hovering in double-digits. Had the United States not acted as an external spur to West European economic expansion, the subsequent resumption of growth in the region during the mid-1980s might not have occurred.

For the debt-ridden economies of the developing world, America's import markets were even more critical in averting potential disaster. Having accumulated nearly $1 trillion in out-

standing foreign liabilities, many indebted countries in Latin
America, Asia, and Africa lacked the requisite foreign exchange
earnings to meet their debt service obligations under adverse
conditions of high international interest rates, declining commodity prices, and kited oil-import bills. With over one-half of
their external debts slated for repayment in U.S. dollars, these
overborrowed countries were confronted with the choice of increasing their exports to the United States or ultimately being
called into default by their external creditors. Between 1983 and
1985, the United States accepted an average of $100 billion an-
nually in export deliveries from these nations, enabling them to
reap $35 billion to $40 billion a year in precious foreign exchange
earnings, much of it earmarked for loan remittances to U.S.-
based banks.[1] Indeed, the importance of the United States to the
debt-strapped Third World is amply evident when we consider
that by 1984, America took a full 58 percent of their total manufactured exports.[2] Absent the willingness of the United States
to run successive trade deficits with these nations, an international financial crisis might well have taken place, plunging the
entire world into a deep depression.

The inflow of external capital which allowed the United States
to incur its large trade deficits with Japan and, to a lesser extent,
Western Europe, performed some useful ancillary functions, albeit temporary ones carrying heavy future costs. To some, the
very existence of this influx can be read as a positive sign in the
sense that the United States was regarded by foreigners as an
attractive investment center offering both safety and comparatively high rates of return.[3] More concretely, in light of America's inordinately low national savings rate and the investment
gap associated with it, "We have had more investment in this
country than we would have without the inflow of capital,"[4] a
portion of these funds going to finance the expansion of production capacity. By the same token, if the federal government's
budget deficits had been met exclusively by internal private savings, domestic interest rates would have been far higher than
they were as the result of intensified competition for available
capital.[5] Thus, by directly or indirectly filling the American government's financing needs, foreign capital transfers to the United
States helped to alleviate pressure on domestic credit markets.[6]

Since the movement of foreign savings into U.S. assets was

the proximate cause of the strong dollar, this flow played a positive part in keeping domestic inflation rates below those which could normally have been expected in an economy featuring robust economic growth. The strong dollar effectively lowered the price of imported goods and services and created dampening pressures on domestically produced items competing with them. It also reduced the dollar-denominated cost of imported raw and semifinished materials used as inputs in domestic production processes, thereby allowing for lower prices on finished goods.[7] Finally, through its mediating effect on American interest rates, capital flows from abroad reduced the cost of capital to American business, part of which would otherwise have been passed down in higher prices to consumers.

While all of the benefits of the American trade imbalance inventoried thus far are now, or will soon become, liabilities, there is a trend brought about by some of our bilateral deficits which will serve to mitigate the strictures of trade-related adjustment in the future. This development concerns the rapid growth of direct investment in the United States by Japanese (and other) multinational corporations. Compared with the United States or Western Europe, Japan has not matched its flow of exports with a correspondingly large volume of direct investment capital. While conglomerates from other nations of the industrialized world have been establishing manufacturing facilities around the globe, with, for example, large American firms typically undertaking 15 percent to 20 percent of their production offshore, Japanese companies generate an average of less than 4 percent of their output through overseas production.[8] Between 1951 and 1972, Japanese direct investment in the United States and Canada amounted to a miniscule $303 million, with another $3.5 billion occurring between 1973 and 1982.[9] However, between 1981 and 1983, total Japanese direct investment tripled, with the United States being the major recipient,[10] and by March 1984, Japanese manufacturing facilities in the United States reached a value of $16.5 billion.[11] Presently, more than 1,800 Japanese firms have subsidiaries operating in the United States.[12] The Japanese government estimates that by the end of the century, increased investment by Japanese enterprises could create some 840,000 new jobs for American workers.[13]

The expansion of Japanese-owned production in America has

come in two stages. In the first, as their country became the main scapegoat for American protectionists, the Japanese moved part of their production capacity to the United States. This offered them a means of securing guaranteed access to American markets and a way of mollifying anti-Japanese protectionist sentiment.[14] In the second phase, with Japan's dollar-denominated labor costs rising on the ascent of the yen, direct investment in the United States by Japanese companies became a cost-reduction strategy, akin to the movement of American multinationals to the developing world in search of inexpensive labor.[15] For both political and purely economic reasons, Japanese firms have been greatly expanding their presence within the American industrial landscape, many participating in joint ventures with established American corporations, for instance, General Motors/Toyota, IBM/Nippon Telephone & Telegraph, etc. Apprehensive about the protectionist consequences of their excessive large bilateral trade surpluses with the United States, South Korean outfits are now setting up shop in America as well. Korean companies such as Gold Star America and Samsung have already established production plants in the United States putting out large volumes of consumer durables.[16] Although Japanese, South Korean, and other foreign investment in the United States is owned by corporations headquartered abroad that will receive profit remittances from their subsidiaries, these activities do create employment for Americans and help offset the growth-retarding effects of America's trade deficits and trade-related debts.

The consolation afforded by the positive effects of the U.S. trade imbalance is of precious little comfort when viewed against the negative outcomes comprising the heart of the monetarist interpretation. From the monetarist perspective, America's trade gap is essentially a balance-of-payments disequilibrium that cannot be sustained in the long run and necessarily entails severe near-term difficulties. In 1981 and the first half of 1982, the United States registered small surpluses ($6 billion a year) in its international current accounts, with net receipts on service transactions and investment income overcoming modest shortfalls in its merchandise trade.[17] Although net service/investment earnings fell during the next three years, the deterioration in our current account to $-46 billion (1983), $-107.4 billion (1984) and $-117.7 billion (1985) was due chiefly to America's eroding trade record.[18] In the first half of 1986, this pattern of expanding current account deficits continued, as official sources reported a $-137.4 billion shortfall on an annualized basis.[19]

By definition, as the United States accumulates current account deficits, this creates a commensurately large stock of outstanding external debt.[20] It is within the framework of its net international investment position that the monetary consequences of America's perennial trade deficits are displayed in their sharpest form. Table 5 reveals a historic shift in the international financial status of the United States. In 1982, America was a very large net creditor country on its international capital account, the nation's investments abroad exceeding foreign investments in the United States by $147 billion. At the end of 1984, this net surplus had dwindled to $28.2 billion, the value of America's overseas assets ($915 billion) being slightly greater than the value of foreign-owned assets in the United States ($886 billion).[21] It was during the first half of 1985, as new foreign investment in America amounted to $40 billion and new American-owned assets in foreign economies came to a mere $5 billion, that the United States became a net-debtor country for the first time since 1914. Updated data show that by the end of 1985, the United States owed a net of $107.44 billion to external investors, giving it the dubious distinction of having the world's largest foreign debt.[22] As a direct outgrowth of our trade deficits, the United States witnessed an international capital surplus built up over more than six decades evaporate in less than three years before turning into an equivalently large deficit.[23] Although its stock of external debt differs fundamentally from those of Third World countries since it is scheduled for repayment in dollars,[24] it must nonetheless be serviced through future export earnings and internal savings.

Examining Table 5 in closer detail, several qualifications are in order regarding the magnitude of our international liabilities. First, the decline of the nation's net direct investment from $97.1 billion in 1982 to $75 billion in 1985 is a rough approximation. Both U.S. direct investment and foreign direct investment in America are expressed at original book values and do not reflect

Table 5
International Investment Position of the United States, 1982–1985 (in dollars billion)

	1982	1983	1984	1985
Total International Investment Position	147.0	106.2	28.2	-60.0
New Direct Investment	97.1	89.9	73.8	75.0
Other Recorded Portfolio, Net	26.1	-11.2	-73.9	-165.0
Gold, SDRs, IMF	23.7	27.5	28.3	30.0
Cumulative Unrecorded Transactions	-109.0	-120.5	-145.2	-175.0
Recorded Position Plus Cumulative Unreported Transactions	38.0	-14.3	-117.0	-235.0

Source: Robert A. Johnson, "U.S. International Transactions in 1985," _Federal Reserve Bulletin_, vol. lxxii, no. 5 (May, 1986), p. 294.

either physical depreciation or inflation-induced asset appreciation.[25] Next, our stock of government gold reserves (260 million ounces) is assessed in these figures at $42 per ounce or $11 billion, when its current market value is, in fact, about ten times that sum.[26] The positive news of undervalued gold holdings, however, is more than negated by the $175 billion deficit in cumulative unrecorded transactions. In prepearing international accounts, American statisticians, like their counterparts elsewhere, discover that some cross-border capital transactions are erroneously valued while others are simply unreported. Such errors and omissions appear in balance-of-payments ledgers as a discrepancy between reported transactions and net changes in international monetary accounts. The main source of the enormous $175 billion in cumulative unrecorded transactions reckoned on this basis seems to be hidden capital inflows, so-called capital flight money sent by private foreign citizens from their countries to the United States. In essence, the statistical discrepancy in America's balance-of-payments capital account is due to large sums of foreign assets in the United States not registered as foreign-owned. If this is the case, "then U.S. net international indebtedness is significantly greater than is specifically reported in the account and the U.S. became a net debtor" prior to June 1985.[27] All in all, by the end of 1985, America was probably deeper in debt than its official books show by between $75 billion and $100 billion.

As of the third quarter of 1986, the United States still receives more in income from its overseas investments than it pays to foreigners because many of our older assets carry a higher rate of return than more recent foreign investments in U.S. assets.[28] Nonetheless, since the United States continues to post ever-larger current account deficits, America is on the cusp of sending more in interest/dividend payments to others than we receive, so that our current account imbalance will soon be larger than our merchandise trade deficit. Without a radical turnabout in our trade performance, both our current account shortfalls and our net international indebtedness will snowball. C. Fred Bergstein estimates that by 1990 yearly U.S. current account deficits will reach $300 billion and our net international debt will surpass $1 trillion.[29] America's ascent to its capital account pinnacle of mid-

1982 required more than six decades of laborious effort, but once the descent started, future indebtedness took on the momentum of past borrowings.

The unavoidable result of America's trade-related external debt is a further slowdown in the already flagging pace of U.S. outgrowth. In theory, a nation can prudently accept debt-creating capital flows from an external source in much the same manner as a private company can contract a loan from a bank. This recourse to debt is sound if enough of those credits are channeled into productive investments capable of generating increased earnings which can be used to repay the original loan. Regrettably, it is in their common violation of this discipline that the analogy between American and Third World foreign debts rings true. The capital inflows accompanying our trade deficits, like the cross-border loans made to developing nations, were used primarily to finance current consumption, not productive investment, chiefly "public spending with little or no future economic yield."[30] The result is that the United States (like many Third World debtors) must service its international obligations without the compensatory benefit of externally funded productivity increases. Estimating just how severe this debt drag on future output expansion will be (and when it will reach full force) hinges largely upon which of the broad adjustment paths we shall be examining shortly takes place. According to one forecast in line with Bergstein's calculations, servicing $1 trillion in external debt by 1990 would slash America's GNP growth by a full two percentage points a year.[31]

Precisely how the future recessionary impact of America's trade deficits will unfold depends upon how foreign investors react to prospective remedial policies adopted by United States monetary authorities. For the sake of simplifying an extraordinary complex web of interpenetrating influences, let us assume that little relief will be forthcoming from federal budget-cutting or improved private savings rates. In response to the nation's growing trade imbalance, the chief policy instrument available to the Federal Reserve Board is located in its control over the discount rate. By cutting the cost of funds to the country's banks, the Fed can prompt a decline in interest rates on U.S. investments thereby (a) making American assets less attractive to foreign investors and (b) placing downward pressure on the dollar, which, in turn, will restore price competitiveness to American goods and services in world markets. Both of these outcomes will help to bring the nation's merchandise trade account into equilibrium, but the intentional curbing of foreign capital inflows also mean that such investment as does take place in the United States must be increasingly sourced from America's internal savings.

Suppose that foreign investors, particularly the Japanese, elect to merely decrease their capital transfers to the United States. With the total available investment capital reduced, domestic interest rates will subsequently rise, retarding growth in the American economy as a whole and especially in interest-sensitive sectors such as housing.[32] Because high rates of interest are one of the main targets of corrective action by the Fed in the first place, the Fed could pump up the money supply through further rate cuts at the risk of future price inflation and interest rate increases. This "soft landing" scenario, then, features a gradual reduction in foreign purchases of American assets, with U.S. monetary officials walking a tightrope between short-term adjustment policies to redress the trade imbalance and their self-negation in the long term. In this context, the growth-inhibiting effects of accumulated foreign debt will take place slowly, but they will be accompanied by an elongated devaluation-inflation spiral.

The alternative hard landing scenario differs from its soft counterpart in that foreign investors do not simply curb their outflow of savings to the United States, they also withdraw funds previously placed in American assets. Should our external creditors lose basic confidence in the U.S. economy, this would lead to a precipitous plunge in the dollar's value.[33] The combined effect of hasty capital withdrawal and a sharp depreciation of the dollar might well provoke a financial crisis in the United States. As the panic evolves, even extraordinarily high domestic interest rates will not restore capital formation to a level sufficient to meet our ongoing internal and external debt-service needs. Hence, there will be virtually no money available for investment in private enterprise, the federal government will be compelled to reduce growth-stimulating expenditures and the American economy will contract at a rapid pace. In contrast to the soft landing trajectory, the impact of accumulated external debt upon American GNP growth would be more abrupt and, initially, more severe.

Evaluating the relative probabilities of these projected courses, the soft scenario appears far more likely to occur than the hard line plunge. When we examine the composition of foreign-owned assets in the United States, we find a number of obstacles to a swift retreat of foreign capital. Approximately one-fifth of all foreign-owned assets in the United States are held by official agencies abroad. These bodies are unlikely to reduce their holdings of dollar-denominated assets at a time when the dollar is weakening of its own accord, since this would impinge upon the price competitiveness of their exports and import-competing items. Another one-quarter of foreign-owned assets are in the form of direct investments in physical assets in the United States. It would require some time to liquidate these, especially under presumed conditions of tight credit markets. U.S. stocks and bonds in foreign portfolios could be disposed of more readily (such holdings amounting to 28 percent of total foreign assets), but a broad withdrawal from these instruments would require that investors sell at a time of sharp price declines. Comprising the final quarter of all foreign-owned investments in the United States, claims against American banks, for example, money market deposits, might be retracted with comparative ease, but the Fed could counterbalance this withdrawal through a relatively modest expansion of the money supply.[34]

Another argument on behalf of a soft landing is evident when we look at the wherewithal of foreign investors. For example, as of mid-1985, the investment portfolios of Japanese institutions totalled $3.8 trillion, of which just 2 percent, or $76 billion, was in the form of foreign securities, chiefly U.S. Government Treasury notes. If these institutions were to place but 10 percent of their available funds into American assets, over $300 billion in additional monies would be poised to flow into the United States. These funds *alone* could support present U.S. current account deficits for two or three years.[35]

Lastly, if Japanese and other foreign investors have a mind to drastically reduce their exposures in the United States, they have not demonstrated this intention to date. During the U.S. Treasury's 28 billion quarterly refunding auction of August 1986, Japanese nationals purchased ten-year and thirty-year bonds at about the same participation rate (one-third of the total) as they did during the previous spring's offering.[36]

The apparent willingness of foreigners to increase their holdings of American assets (at least) in the near term brings us to a third variation in the monetarist version of the trade deficit's impact upon American growth. This scenario differs from those previously described in that it is already under way. Its basic point is that even *if* foreign investors elect to continue to send savings into American assets at about the same pace as in the immediate past, the trade imbalance has still caused a growth slowdown in the United States which will soon be accompanied by rising inflation and domestic interest rates. In a sense, the monetarist analysis of the trade deficit's meanings incorporates many of the same phenomena as the structuralist interpretation of its origins, simply reversing the direction of causality.[37] Hence, it has been argued: "It is not that productivity weakness caused our trade problems, but that the trade problems caused the decline in productivity."[38] As American and foreign consumers rejected U.S.-made goods in favor of those offered by our trade competitors, U.S. export and import-competing corporations were deprived of potential sales earnings. In turn, with corporate revenues receding, their capital outlays have been reduced. This, of course, serves to undermine productivity growth, and, with it, overall GNP expansion.

At the start of 1986, the Reagan administration predicted a partial return to the buoyant GNP growth rates of 1983 and 1984, forecasting a national output advance of 4 percent during the year.[39] Declining interest rates and, most especially, ebbing oil prices lent some credence to this optimistic projection, but during the first six months of the year, America's GNP growth plodded along at a pace of 2.2 percent.[40] According to Federal Reserve Board Chairman Paul Volcker, the principal cause of continued lackluster GNP growth in the United States was the trade deficit itself.[41] American consumers and corporations employed the additional buying power brought about by low interest rates and oil prices to continue their import-buying spree, and, consequently, roughly one-half of the growth which would have occurred under these favorable conditions was drained into foreign economies.

A general consensus has emerged that the trade deficit itself (that is, apart from trade-related debt) has chopped between 1 and 2 percentage points of potential growth from the American economy in each year since 1982,[42] this effect increasing to over 2 percentage points in 1986.[43] In the summer of 1986, with the trade deficit bounding along at a record clip, America's industrial production dropped for three straight months, the nation's factories operating at 78.2 percent of capacity in July.[44] As foreign goods have supplanted American-made wares in domestic and external markets, American manufacturers have been compelled to cut production in line with reduced demand. Thus, from the monetarist standpoint, it is the worsening of America's trade performance per se which has forced American firms to slash their capital spending plans in 1986, since they lack the sales earnings to undertake new investments and sufficient prospective demand to warrant greater recourse to external financing.

Under normally favorable conditions, the American economy can be expected to grow at a pace of 3 percent to 4 percent a year. Should conditions remain basically as they are, by 1990 the United States will find its growth rate pared by 2 percentage points as a consequence of repayment on trade-related external debt *and* an additional 2 percentage points as a result of the concurrent annual trade deficit! The obvious inference, then, is that absent strong corrective action, the trade imbalance and attendant debt will reduce American GNP growth to zero or less by the end of the 1980s.

The second broad influence which the American trade deficit will have, from the monetarist perspective, resides in its impact upon domestic price inflation. Much to the monetarists' puzzlement, a sharp rise in inflation, unlike laggard output growth, has yet to occur in the United States. Of course, some peripheral forces continue to hold prices down, e.g., sagging petroleum prices, weak commodity markets, and (temporarily) easy credit terms resulting from the Fed's accommodationist policies. However, from the monetarist standpoint, higher inflation rates will rear up in the United States independent of the Fed's policies and potential changes in foreign investment flows. As the value of the dollar has already begun to decline to levels more reflective of America's declining economic health, currency depreciation will eventually generate a sharp upward movement in American price inflation. On this count, Richard Cooper informs us:

The inflation gains that the United States "borrowed" from the future when the dollar appreciated so sharply have to be repaid. It is usually estimated that each 10 percent real depreciation of the dollar will lead eventually to increases in the consumer price index of 1 to 2 percent.[45]

According to C. Fred Bergstein, dollar devaluation of 20 percent a year for two years—the approximate pace of the dollar's decline against G-10 currencies since February 1985—will lift price inflation in the United States from its 2.5 percent to 3 percent range in 1986 to a level of 7 percent per annum or higher by 1988.[46]

There are at least three conduits through which a weakening dollar will spur inflation in the United States. First, an eroding dollar necessarily means a decline in terms of trade for the United States relative to economies with currencies appreciating against it. The dollar-denominated price of imported goods, services, and production inputs from these countries will eventually rise to mirror currency realignments. Some of the demand for imports will shift to homespun items, but some imports are either essential (e.g., petroleum), or have no domestic substitutes (e.g., video recorders). Second, the downward movement of the dollar will cause foreign investors to demand a currency exchange risk premium on their U.S. assets. Hence, even if they are willing to send America funds at the same rate as in the past, foreign investors will require higher rates of return to compensate for foreign exchange movements. The resulting rise in interest rates will have a mutually reinforcing relationship with domestic inflation rates so that, for instance, increased capital costs for American manufacturers will be built into prices on finished wares. Third, as the nation's terms of trade deteriorate and higher interest rates lend additional force to domestic price inflation, American workers will experience a pronounced drop in their real purchasing power. This will press them to demand higher wages to offset existing inflation, pushing consumer prices still higher.[47] Given all this, we find Fed chairman Volcker's mid-1986 threat to let the dollar fall further if our major trading partners fail to institute discount rate cuts inherently undermined. Both Volcker and our trade rivals know full well that a further drop in the dollar's value will ultimately cause even higher American inflation rates in the future than those already predetermined by the dollar's decline to date.[48]

It is exceedingly difficult to imagine a more negative set of conditions besetting the American economy than those encompassed by the growth/inflation effects of the trade deficit from the monetarist standpoint. Nevertheless, there is another potential development arising from the U.S. trade imbalance which could exacerbate current and future stagflation. Harried by lobbyists from import-competing industries, American congresspersons have bowed to these provincial interests by presenting a wide array of protectionist legislation for enactment into law. As we shall discover in the next chapter, there is some question about whether these office-holders actually believe in the protectionist arguments proffered by their constituents, but even lacking a sincere conviction about this course, a majority of American congresspersons have voted for new or intensified import barriers. In 1985, more than 300 separate bills calling for heightened tariffs, strengthened nontariff barriers, and reduced import quotas were afoot on Capitol Hill.[49] The rationale behind these proposals is that (1) America's bilateral trade deficits are the product of unfair trading policies by foreign governments and (2) large bilateral imbalances are *prima facie* proof of these underhanded practices at work. Whether Congress will succeed in putting these measures into operation is still very much in doubt: Thus far, a free market Reagan administration has forestalled the protectionist surge through a combination of presidential vetoes and piecemeal retaliatory actions against the most objectionable cases of export promotion/import restriction abroad.

From the monetarist perspective, acceding to this misguided protectionist upswell would merely exacerbate America's trade-related woes. If additional fences were to be erected around the American economy, our already eroding competitiveness will suffer an even sharper downturn. On the broadest front, protectionist relief granted to domestic industries harmed by import competition distorts the nation's internal allocation of resources, shifting them from relatively efficient enterprises to comparatively inefficient ones. Bolstering the performance of protected industries through import constraints lends these producers an unwarranted advantage against other *domestic* industries competing against them for capital, labor, and technology, in effect, sacrificing a measure of the latter's competitiveness in support of the former's noncompetitiveness.[50] Since protectionism enables favored industries to keep prices on their products at levels higher than they would be in an open market environment, disfavored or neglected domestic businesses must pay this cost, again reducing their natural competitiveness.[51] For example, in December 1985, the International Trade Commission found that a proposed program to restrain steel imports would cost *American exporters* of steel-containing products over $15 billion in increased material costs and lost sales.[52] In the monetarist understanding, the old saw of "robbing Peter to pay Paul" is a fundamental truism insofar as the purely *domestic impact* of protectionism is concerned.

The monetarist indictment of protectionism continues further, extending to the protected industries themselves. Once braced by shields against foreign competition, these favored industries are deprived of a stimulus for enhancing their own performance. In his survey of European firms adjusting to low-cost foreign competition, Robert Grant observed that the "greatest productivity gains [occurred] among firms which were subject to strong import competition at a comparatively early stage."[53] Those producers who enjoy relief from foreign imports ultimately find themselves dependent upon artificial policy devices for their very survival. "Analysis of a sample of sixteen industries" in the United States "that received some type of import protection over the last two decades indicates that only one of them, the bicycle industry, increased its production and employment levels after protectionism was removed,"[54] while the remainder shrank in size. If protectionism takes the form of tariff increases, this may merely provide foreign suppliers with a further impetus to upgrade their production efficiency. If protectionism takes the form of import quotas, this furnishes foreign producers with fattened profit margins, strengthens their largest firms through industry consolidation, and prompts them to ratchet up to the luxury end of the American market.[55]

Lastly, apart from its counterproductive impact on American industries competing for national resources, and, ironically, those receiving import protection, such trade impediments undermine the overall global competitiveness of the United States.

Import protection would initially worsen the trade balances of the countries against whom it was directed. As a result, their currencies would tend to depreciate against the dollar. In turn, this would impair the competitive position of American export industries, which, by their very nature, are likely to be the leading edge of economic progress.[56]

Aside from reducing the ability of our trading partners to purchase American-made goods and strangling the debt-service capacity of many developing countries, our own protectionist devices "would strengthen the dollar and reduce the competitiveness of American goods in world markets."[57] We shall again encounter the protectionist outburst in the United States as part of the structuralist interpretation of the trade deficit's meanings. This alternative viewpoint stresses the deleterious impact of increased American trade barriers upon American consumers, and so, it differs from the monetarist emphasis upon reduced internal and external economic efficiency. In their broad assessments, however, the two sides offer the same summary judgment: Attempting to alleviate the influence of foreign competition upon American industries via protectionist means will simply magnify our trade-related problems and make them far more intractable to affirmative policy responses.

THE STRUCTURALIST POSITION

Concentrating on real factors at the microeconomic level, the structuralist version of the meanings of the U.S. trade imbalance contains a much shorter list of benefits than its monetarist counterpart. With the exception of its use as a spur to reform in industry practice, the structuralists see the trade deficit as a wholly negative phenomenon. The core of the structuralist interpretation of the trade gap's consequences is nothing less than a fundamental and permanent devolution in the structure of the American economy. Competition from foreign products in American and external markets will inevitably lead to the deindustrialization of the United States. Our basic capital-intensive smokestack industries will be progressively dismantled under the force of low-cost competition from abroad. This process is already proceeding apace in such sunset industries as steel and textiles, where plant closings and workforce cuts are now commonplace. Some of this industrial capacity has been transplanted offshore by American multinational corporations that have moved large portions of their operations to foreign climes. No matter what changes occur in macroeconomic conditions, the structuralists maintain that most of this lost industrial activity will not return home.

What, then, will take the place of these manufacturing facilities? The structuralists observe that an increasing portion of America's economic activity will be converted into service functions as the United States becomes the world's first, post-industrial service economy. Unfortunately, reliance upon services as the backbone of the American economy will mean lower productivity increases, reduced wage scales, and declining living standards since services generally underperform manufacturing on all of these counts. Moreover, the service sector is inherently limited in its potential for growth absent a strong domestic manufacturing sector and it will prove more difficult for the United States to redress its trade balance through an expansion of service exports compared to manufactured goods. We cannot, however, resort to import restraints to slow deindustrialization and obviate its negative outgrowths. The protectionist recourse advocated by an increasing legion of public and private spokesmen will not restore the nation's industries to a sound footing. According to the structuralists, protectionism will simply invite retaliation from America's trade partners and raise the cost of goods in domestic markets.

The lone benefit of the current U.S. trade deficit from the structuralist angle is that it has unmistakably demonstrated the degree to which American producers have lagged behind the advances of their foreign rivals in the mobilization and management of production factors. Whether they attribute their failing ability to meet the foreign production challenge to unfair trade practices or to a basic competitiveness gap, American corporations are now compelled to adjust their own operations. As their market shares have contracted under the onslaught of foreign goods, producers in the United States have been pressured "to adopt more efficient techniques to modernize and to cut costs, to innovate and to invest in productivity enhancements to compete with the foreign producers."[58] As noted in Chapter 2, although many American firms have taken a defensive, cost-reduction approach to adjustment, others, albeit far fewer, have instituted aggressive progams of product/process innovation as attested to by the burgeoning of corporate research and development outlays in the mid-1980s.[59] Without the fresh wind of foreign competition prodding them to alter their tired ways, American manufacturers may have remained content to follow their inefficient practices at a broad cost to the national economy and increased vulnerability to future external challenges. Our eroding trade performance, then, has carried a loud message about the ill-health of American enterprise, and it is this call to necessary reform that comprises the beginning and the end of its positive connotation in the structuralist argument.

In the context of the U.S. trade imbalance, the structuralists' deindustrialization thesis is vague in its distinction between cause and effect. The long-standing declines in America's erstwhile factor advantages covered in Chapter 2 clearly contributed to the deindustrialization process before the advent of large trade deficits. Hence, the damage inflicted by the nation's declining trade performance on our industrial base was as much an acceleration of existing trends as an independent causal factor.[60] On the other hand, our industrial decline does owe much to the increased foreign competition reflected in our trade accounts since 1980. Since that time, the bulk of our yearly trade gaps have been largely the result of a sectoral weakening in manufactures, especially in those older industries in which the United States enjoyed absolute supremacy less than two decades ago. Since 1984, manufacturing output in the United States has shown zero growth as imports have captured most of the marginal increase in demand for manufactured goods in American markets. Indeed, the production output of America's factories, mines, and utilities during the second quarter of 1986 was substantially below that of the second quarter of 1985,[61] and spare capacity in the country's production facilities has risen to above 20 percent. Moreover, while service sector employment has mushroomed since 1980, the number of American manufacturing jobs has actually declined.[62] All of this is taken as clear-cut evidence of the deindustrialization process within the American economy by the structuralists. As Milton Hochmuth puts it: "There can be no argument that for an industrialized nation to lose market share for its manufactured goods, including an important share of its home market is cause for significant alarm.[63] Outside the framework of international competition, the absolute decline of manufacturing activity in the United States is deemed a negative development since manufacturing activity is considered intrinsically desirable and the shift out of manufacturing and into the service sector entails substantial financial and human costs.

In the structuralist interpretation of the trade deficit's impact, America's basic, capital-intensive, and low-skill industries are often called "key" or "linkage" sectors to underscore their integral part in the country's industrial base as a whole. One of the prime examples of an industry whose decline has rippled through the economy at large is steel. It is not simply the sheer size of steel in terms of its output and employment which lends it the distinction of being a key manufacturing activity. It is the fact that steel serves as a ubiquitous input in the production of a wide spectrum of capital and consumer goods. Consequently, as steel's performance erodes under the weight of foreign competition, a broad portion of the nation's manufacturing sector becomes increasingly dependent upon external suppliers. At present, nearly one-third of all steel consumed in the United States is imported from abroad, and this expansion has been matched by a sharp drop in domestic steel production.[64] One of the industries most closely connected to steel is automobile production, which, quite obviously, consumes a massive amount of steel. Here too we find that import penetration has been generally greater than in other industries, with over one-fourth of all cars sold in the United States today being manufactured by foreign companies.[65] In the most simplified sense, as American steel loses market share and the ability to enhance its productivity, the country's automotive industry undergoes a correlative downshift, while reduced sales of American-made cars dampens demand for domestically produced steel. In turn, as both steel and auto erode, this impacts upon other linkage industries in the American economy, machine tool production, for example, where domestic companies now enjoy less than 50 percent of total sales revenues in American markets.[66]

One of the principal strategies that America's corporate leaders have adopted in response to low-cost foreign imports is the establishment of production facilities abroad. Foreign sourcing of components and finished products has risen dramatically as the U.S. trade gap has grown, this tactic having a self-evident role in America's deindustrialization. In 1984, a survey of 152 American manufacturers found that 77 percent of them had increased their use of overseas sourcing in the previous five years.[67]

This shift to production outside of the United States by American-based companies is an across-the-board trend affecting traditional low-tech industries and high-tech sectors as well. In 1986, 18 percent of the parts embodied in automobiles assembled in the United States were made abroad, and that figure is expected to rise to 29 percent by 1995. In fact, through joint production arrangements with foreign automakers, by 1988, 17 percent of all cars sold by Detroit will be manufactured abroad in their entirety.[68] When American consumers buy a television set bearing the label of a well-known domestic company, the chances are nine in ten that it has been put together in Mexico, Taiwan, Singapore, or some other economy offering cheap assembly line labor.[69] The same trend is underway in the computer field, an area in which the United States is said to retain a comparative cost advantage using purely domestic inputs. In terms of total manufacturing costs, approximately 70 percent of the components that go into IBM's "American-made" computers are sourced offshore.[70] With Japanese companies increasing their production in the United States as American outfits move overseas, there is an overarching irony evident, as increasingly "American consumers will be asked to make a choice between a Sony TV made in the U.S. and a Zenith TV made in foreign countries, or a Honda car made in the U.S. and a Dodge car made in Japan."[71]

It is self-apparent that this defensive, cost-cutting reaction to foreign competition is a basic cause of the increased pace of America's deindustrialization. By transferring facilities abroad, large U.S. corporations hope to reestablish their former cost advantages, chiefly through reduced labor bills. However, from the structuralist standpoint, offshore sourcing will prove to be a self-perpetuating and a self-defeating tactic. Reliance on production overseas temporarily reduces pressure upon American firms to implement productivity-boosting innovations in their remaining plants at home.[72] Examining this loss of innovational push, Stephen Cohen and John Zysman comment: "Earlier moves offshore were often taken without clear attention to the possibilities of traditional automation" and ongoing shifts abroad "may blind firms to the possibilities and need of automating at home"[73] through "new generation" manufacturing techniques. Their decision to pull up stakes at home may well prompt American corporations to neglect the potential productivity gains available through innovation, and, hence, lead them to transfer additional capacity abroad as home-based productivity wanes.

The structuralist argument, moreover, offers a more finely detailed account concerning the cumulative nature of overseas production by American companies. The migration to foreign sourcing evolves in relatively distinct phases, each creating further momentum for the complete abandonment of production in the United States. When an individual firm starts to produce components through foreign subsidiaries, management soon discovers that it makes less and less sense to subsequently ship these parts to the United States for final assembly. Once complete assembly lines are established abroad, the distance between them and management/staff functions becomes a great hindrance. Consequently, as the juggernaut rolls on, this company will move management and technical activities, research and development, for example, to the overseas production site.[74] As the source of intrafirm innovation is exported abroad, headquarters becomes less adept at understanding how new technology can be exploited, and, hence, its ability to undertake innovation at home is undercut. Meanwhile, the foreign subsidiary now recruits a

larger and larger proportion of its managerial and technical personnel from the local populace. Hence, foreign nationals find
their working skills progressively upgraded while those of the
company's home staff begin to slide. In the penultimate stage,
foreign managers and technical personnel leave the American-
owned subsidiary to form their own companies. For instance,
General Instrument Corporation's Taiwan branch now competes
with no less than eleven separate local companies founded by
former employees.[75] In the end, the parent company has created
the conditions of its own demise by (1) allowing its skill base to
atrophy and (2) spawning competition from newly formed foreign outfits manned by individuals with extensive experience.

The fatalism inherent in the structuralist rendition of American industrial erosion through offshore production is but a part
of a major point of disagreement between it and the monetarist
position. The monetarist argument implies that American industrial capacity will somehow "snap back" once a favorable macroeconomic environment arises. For the structuralists, deindustrialization is essentially a one-way street. To begin, "foreign
companies that establish sales, distribution networks and even
brand recognition in the United States market will tend to hold
them as the dollar declines,"[76] using their past profits from sales
in America to strengthen their competitive edge and secure their
foothold in the United States.[77] At the same time, import-competing American firms which shutter capacity and send their
workers home are likely to find themselves at the end of the
road. "Once a plant has been closed, and its machinery auc-
tioned, it rarely makes sense to turn back" and try to restart
production under more favorable macroeconomic conditions.[78]
Thus, without a positive and comprehensive national strategy to
deal with foreign manufacturing competition, America's industrial base will become a thing of the past as the nation loses the
essential know-how to rebuild it in the future.

What will take the place of America as an industrial arsenal in
the structuralist version of the trade deficit's effects is a new
society, a so-called hamburger economy run by short-order cooks,
sales clerks, xerox operators, and messenger boys. Even as
America's industrial strength has been sapped by foreign competition, its service sector has blossomed. Services now account

for 70 percent of America's national output and a like proportion of private sector employment.[79] By the end of the century, it is projected that service's share of American GNP will rise to 85 percent with an equivalent increase in its share of total jobs.[80] We get a rough idea of just how important services have become in the United States relative to manufacturing when we observe that if employment growth in services since 1970 had inched along at the same pace as in manufacturing, the nation's unemployment rate would now be nearing 30 percent.[81] While the measurement of services is a complicated task owing to the amorphous character of this sector,[82] the transformation of the United States into a service-oriented economy is virtually beyond question.

At first blush, the change from heavy manufacturing to service activities does not appear to be a wholly undesirable occurrence. Services are, after all, environmentally clean and occupationally safe compared to traditional industrial operations. Hence, the question logically arises: What is so bad about services, or, in restated form, why not a deindustrialized economy? For openers, services are usually more labor-intensive and less capital-intensive than manufacturing,[83] and they generally feature a lower level of capital investment per worker than industrial production.[84] The problem, then, is that services afford less scope for productivity gains through capital outlays and technological innovations. Indeed the level of productivity in services and the rate of productivity increases in this sector normally trail behind those posted by the manufacturing sector.[85] According to a number of scholars, between one-half and three-quarters of the slowdown in aggregate American productivity growth over the past two decades can be traced to the movement out of manufacturing and into services.[86]

As the American manufacturing sector gradually weakens, the service sector will lose a portion of its most important source of internal demand. Since a support network inherently requires something to support, a service-driven economy must rely upon sales to basic industries in order to grow. Some service industries, such as advertising agencies, are directly linked to manufacturing customers; others, like retail stores, derive a large percentage of their revenue from sales to industrial workers. As it

turns out, General Motors' single largest supplier is not a steel
or a tire producer, but Blue Cross/Blue Shield.[87] Hence, each
time GM cuts back on its workforce as an outcome on foreign
import penetration, Blue Cross/Blue Shield experiences a corresponding loss in its income.

Admittedly, certain services, banking, for example, can compensate for lost sales to American industry by enlarging their
activities overseas. In contrast to merchandise, however, a large
number of services cannot be shipped abroad. Foreign consumers can readily purchase American-made manufactures, but they
will not be sending their dirty clothes to the United States for
dry cleaning. Aside from such intrinsic limitations on the cross-
border movement of services, both industrialized and developing countries impose extensive legal restrictions on foreign-based
services that are, as a rule, more constricting than tariff/nontariff
barriers on merchandise imports. Unlike industrial and agricultural goods, international transactions in services have not received detailed coverage under the General Agreement on Tariffs and Trade (GATT).[88] Although the GATT has not resulted
in a genuinely open global market, its sovereign signatories (including virtually all governments outside of the Eastern Bloc)
are at least nominally committed to liberal treatment of merchandise imports. Without a like umbrella accord governing international services, many potential users are dissuaded from
contracting them by statutory limitations and outright prohibi-
tions. In Japan, U.S. accounting firms are required to submit
their audits of Japanese clients to a Japanese accountant for ver-
ification. U.S. insurance companies operating in France are limited in the type of coverage which they can extend to their French
customers. Italy bans all foreign advertising services from its
economy. The same types of restrictions on services are even
more pronounced in the Third World, with developing countries
steadfastly opposing the extension of GATT-like liberalization to
service imports. Hence, in South Korea, foreign-owned banks
are barred from acquiring title to real estate; Brazil prohibits
foreign insurance companies; Argentina, Mexico, Peru, and
Venezuela all require that foreign accountants be directly super-
vised by their respective nationals.[89] These barriers to services
appear to have had a stronger impact on the United States than

on other net-service exporting nations. Enjoying unrestricted access to other countries within the E.E.C., both Britain and France annually export services equal in value to those of the United States.[90] America's lack of access to service export markets, moreover, appears to have played a part in the decline of the country's share of world exports in special business services, like engineering, from 15 percent in 1973 to just 8 percent in 1983.[91] As an internal source of growth, the performance of services is yoked to the status of domestic manufacturing; as a source of aggregate export growth, services are limited by their nature and by deeply entrenched foreign import barriers.

The shift from manufacturing into services as an element of America's deindustrialization will tend to reinforce the abrasive effects of declining productivity gains, currency depreciation, and external debt-service payments upon American wages and living standards. As American productivity growth lags behind those of our trade rivals, wages in the United States must be adjusted downward for American businesses to stave off a complete competitiveness collapse. As the dollar loses its relative value, real American consumer purchasing power drops accordingly. As national resources are transferred abroad to repay trade-related debt, less physical output is available for current domestic consumption. At the same time, as American workers are shifted from manufacturing to service jobs, their pay checks will shrink. On average, private sector service work offers an hourly wage rate 11 percent lower than manufacturing and, on the whole, service jobs feature shorter work weeks and a greater proportion of part-time positions than manufacturing.[92] Beginning in the 1970s, as the American baby boom generation reached working age, more women left the household to enter the labor force and the two-income family became the norm in American society. This demographic change kept United States per capita income rising, but it masked the fact that real income per *worker* decreased as more individuals took lower-paying trade and service jobs.[93]

The impact of this ongoing sectoral shift upon real wages in the United States is an integral part of a larger development directly related to the impact of foreign competition by the structuralists. Between 1960 and 1984, real domestic wages in the

United States increased at a much slower pace than in the economies of our chief trade competitors. Over that span, real wages
in all sectors of the American economy rose a mere 17 percent,
while E.E.C. wages advanced 133 percent and Japanese wages
grew by 160 percent.[94] The shift from manufacturing jobs into
service employment explains part of this comparative decline in
total American wage rates, but that is only half the story. As
displayed in Table 6, within the manufacturing sector itself, the
hourly earnings of American workers trailed advances in Japan
and the European community between 1960 and 1979, and they
declined in absolute terms between 1979 and 1984. Two forces
combined in the decline of compensation rates in the American
manufacturing sector. First, as previously suggested, in order to
compensate for the relative productivity slowdown of the U.S.
industrial sector, manufacturing wages in industries facing strong
import competition (such as auto, steel, and consumer electronics) were adjusted downward to relieve employers of a part of
their labor cost disadvantage. This partially accounts for the pay
freezes and wage givebacks which occurred during the 1980s in
industries heavily affected by import competition. Second, as
foreign manufacturers captured increasing shares of markets in
high-paying industries, American manufacturing workers were

Table 6
**U.S., Japanese, and European Economic Community Hourly Earnings in
Manufacturing Sectors, 1960–1984 (annual average percentage rates of
increase)**

	1960-68	1968-73	1973-79	1979-84
E.E.C.	4.1	4.9	3.5	1.6
Japan	5.2	9.7	1.6	1.5
United States	1.6	1.2	0.0	-0.6

Source: John D.A. Cuddy, "Some Reflections on Growth on
         OECD Economies," Trade and Development, no. 6 (1985),
         p. 49.

forced into lower-paying industrial work.[95] The downturn in U.S. wages caused by our eroding export/import-competing performance reflects American workers being bumped down into both service employment and lower-paying manufacturing jobs. Thus, part and parcel with the deindustrialization of the United States, our worsening trade performance has caused the real purchasing power of American workers to fall on a secular basis.

Although their argument against the use of protectionist devices to stem imports focuses on a different set of consequences, the structuralists are as adamantly opposed to American protectionism as the monetarists. To the monetarist critique of protectionism, the structuralists add that (a) retalitory trade restrictions are ineffective as a weapon against allegedly unfair behavior by foreign governments and (b) trade restrictions carry a disbenefit in higher consumer prices within the United States far greater than its output/employment benefits.

As we shall discover in Chapter 4, the use of protectionist measures to compel other nations to open their economies to American goods or reduce export subsidy programs has proven extremely questionable on a purely practical basis.[96] The shortcomings of protectionist retaliations are apparent when we look at how a typical trade conflict between the United States and a foreign government evolves. Suppose, for example, that American trade officials accept the claims of, say, the motorcycle industry, that a foreign power is unfairly dumping its motorcycles in U.S. markets through subsidy payments to private producers. The claim is characteristically denied by the offending nation and, unable to come to a negotiated agreement, the American government slaps a counterbalancing import surcharge on these motorcycles. This, in turn, prompts an irate foreign government to impose its own import surcharge on a totally unrelated item, American-made semiconductors, for example, damaging an industry which had nothing whatsoever to do with the original complaint. The semiconductor industry, of course, rightfully petitions for redress, calling for a surcharge on semiconductor imports from the foreign nation, and on and on it goes, with the number of affected parties increasing, all suffering, and none attaining a fair resolution. Examples of this sort are legion. To cite just one, in 1983, American textile manufacturers petitioned the

U.S. International Trade Commission to lower quotas on textile imports from mainland China. When their request was granted, the Chinese government responded by canceling orders for the purchase of American wheat. The result: American farmers lost $500 million in export sales as they bore the cost of bracing American textile manufactures against foreign competition.

Apart from being ineffective, recourse to trade restrictions entails an extraordinarily burdensome cost in the form of increased consumer prices in the economy being protected. Tariffs, quotas, and the like enable "relieved" manufacturers to set prices well above those which their wares could command if they were competing with imports on a level basis. It has been estimated that the Voluntary Restraint Agreement on Japanese automobile exports to the United States alone costs American consumers $4 billion a year. Consequently, for each domestic auto job saved, American consumers pay out $160,000 a year, four times the average annual compensation to individual workers in the industry.[97] Each year, import controls in the textile/apparel industry cost American consumers $27 billion ($42,000 per job), in dairy products, $5.5 billion ($220,000 per job), and in benzoid chemical production, $2.7 billion ($1 million per job).[98] As a form of sales tax, moreover, tariffs are highly regressive, falling most heavily upon low-income consumers,[99] while the same inequitable distribution of the tax burden occurs in the case of import quotas.[100]

CONCLUSION

Given its underlying theoretical orientation, it is by no means unexpected that the monetarist version of the trade deficit's meanings should concentrate upon its macroeconomic effects. Trade-related debt and current/future trade imbalances are expressed in reduced output growth and increased domestic inflation within the United States in the monetarist interpretation. The alternative structuralist analysis of the trade deficit's consequences focuses upon changes in the structure of American production caused or intensified by it. Under the weight of foreign competition, the nation's industrial base is eroding, with a service-dominated economy featuring lower productivity, declining real wages, and strong constraints upon future export growth appearing in its stead.

From both perspectives, the impact of America's worsening trade performance will be felt for years, if not decades, to come. However, the monetarist position maintains that slower domestic growth brought about by the trade deficit will eventually lead to the reestablishment of internal/external equilibrium which will serve as a lower level platform for sustainable improvements in the long run. The structuralists reject this notion of a self-correcting mechanism within the trade imbalance. For them, each downward step forced by lost global competitiveness is just that, as both current performance and the capacity to stage a future recovery are undermined. Thus, for the monetarists, the results of the trade deficit may prove long-lived, but they are simply a part of an inexorable cycle: For the structuralists, the trade deficit's effect assumes the form of a straight line downhill.

The divergent viewpoints on the meanings of the U.S. trade deficit presented in this chapter help us to comprehend the radical differences separating monetarists from structuralists on the matter of an appropriate policy response to it. As we shall discover in Chapter 4, the monetarists advocate measures that will initially reinforce the effects of the trade deficit, e.g., growth-cutting fiscal and monetary austerity policies. On the other hand, the structuralists argue for a complete overhaul in the way in which national resources are managed as a means for directly combating the deindustrialization syndrome. Ironically, both sides are dissatisfied with the actual response of the U.S. government to the trade deficit as it now stands. Neither the monetarist nor the structuralist program has been followed by the Reagan administration, and, as to Congress, its reaction to the trade deficit has been to pursue a course rejected by monetarists and structuralists alike, trade-restricting protectionism.

NOTES

1. George Marotta, "Our Domestic and International Deficits," *Vital Speeches*, vol. lii, no. 8 (February 1, 1986), p. 236.

2. Malcolm Baldridge, "Secretary Baldridge Urges Japan to Lower Trade Barriers," *Business America*, vol. ix, no. 16 (August 4, 1986), p. 5.

3. Paul A. Volcker, "Facing Up to the Twin Deficits," *Challenge*, vol. xxvii, no. 1 (March–April 1984), p. 7.

4. Preston Martin, "Statement . . . Before the Subcommittee on Economic Stabilization of the Committee on Banking, Finance and Urban Affairs, U.S. House of Representatives, July 18, 1985," *Federal Reserve Bulletin*, vol. lxxi, no. 9 (September 1985), p. 669.

5. Ibid., p. 698.

6. Volcker, p. 6.

7. Martin, p. 698.

8. *Economist*, April 26, 1986, p. 86.

9. Kiyohiko Fukushima, "Japan's Real Trade Policy," *Foreign Policy*, no. 59 (Summer 1985), p. 23.

10. Inoguchi Takashi, "Japan's Images and Options: Not a Challenger, but a Supporter," *The Journal of Japanese Studies*, vol. xii, no. 1 (Winter 1986), p.106.

11. Fukushima, p. 23.

12. *New York Times*, August 9, 1986, p. 31.

13. Ibid.

14. Fukushima, p. 22.

15. *New York Times*, June 5, 1986, p. D-7.

16. *New York Times*, August 31, 1986, p. A-20.

17. Edward M. Bernstein, "The United States as an International Debtor Country," *The Brookings Review*, vol. iv, no. 1 (Fall 1985), p. 31.

18. Robert A. Johnson, "U.S. International Transactions in 1985," *Federal Reserve Bulletin*, vol. lxxii, no. 5 (May 1986), p. 295.

19. *New York Times*, September 17, 1986, p. D-2.

20. Richard N. Cooper, "Dealing with the Trade Deficit in a Floating Rate System," *Brookings Papers on Economic Activity*, no. 1 (1986), p. 197.

21. Bernstein, p. 28.

22. *New York Times*, September 17, 1986, p. D-2.

23. C. Fred Bergstein, "The Trade Deficit Could Be Ruinous," *Fortune*, vol. cxii, no. 3 (August 5, 1985), p. 105.

24. Martin, p. 699.

25. Ibid.

26. Ibid.

27. Johnson, p. 294.

28. *New York Times*, September 17, 1986, p. D-2.

29. C. Fred Bergstein, "The U.S.–Japan Trade Imbroglio," *Challenge*, vol. xxviii, no. 3 (July–August 1985), p. 14.

30. Cooper, p. 197.

31. *New York Times*, August 1, 1986, p. D-2.

32. Volcker, p. 6.

33. Takashi, p. 104.

34. Bernstein, p. 34.

35. Lawrence Minard, "Noah's Ark, Anyone?" *Forbes*, vol. cxxxvi, no. 4 (August 12, 1985), p. 80.

36. *New York Times*, August 4, 1986, p. D-1.

37. Bernstein, p. 31.

38. *New York Times*, August 17, 1986, p. F-3.

39. *Nation's Business* (September 1986), p. 10.

40. *New York Times*, September 19, 1986, p. D-1.

41. *New York Times*, July 30, 1986, p. D-1.

42. *Nation's Business* (September 1986), p. 10.

43. *New York Times*, July 31, 1986, p. A-1.

44. *New York Times*, August 19, 1986, p. D-1.

45. Cooper, p. 205.

46. Bergstein, "The Trade Deficit Could Be Ruinous," p. 106.

47. Aloysius Ehrbar, "Toppling the Dollar Could Cost a Lot," *Fortune*, vol. cxii, no. 9, p. 25.

48. *Economist*, July 26, 1986, p. 77.

49. Marotta, p. 236.

50. Rachel McCulloch, "Point of View: Trade Deficits, Industrial Competitiveness and the Japanese," *California Management Review*, vol. xxvii, no. 2 (Winter 1985), p. 154.

51. Ibid., p. 155.

52. Paula Stern, "The U.S. Trade System and the National Interest," *Vital Speeches*, vol. lii, no. 13 (April 15, 1986), p. 390.

53. Grant, p. 89.

54. Robert Z. Lawrence and Robert E. Litan, "Living with the Trade Deficit: Adjustment Strategies to Preserve Free Trade," *The Brookings Review*, vol. iv, no. 1 (Fall, 1985) p. 7.

55. Murray L. Weidenbaum, "Freeing Trade," *Beyond the Status Quo: Policy Proposals for America*, ed. David Boaz and Edward H. Crane (Washington: Cato Institute, 1985), p. 94.

56. Charles L. Schultze, "Industrial Policy: A Dissent," *Brookings Review*, vol. ii, no. 1 (Fall 1983), p. 9.

57. Lawrence and Litan, p. 3.

58. Martin, p. 698.

59. Murray L. Weidenbaum, "Learning to Compete: The Outlook for the 1990s," *Vital Speeches*, vol. lii, no. 21 (August 15, 1986), p. 656.

60. Robert Z. Lawrence, "The Myth of U.S. Deindustrialization," *Challenge*, vol. xxvi, no. 5, p. 12.

61. *New York Times*, July 16, 1986, p. D-3.

62. Martin, p. 698.

63. Milton Hochmuth, "From Challenger to Challenged," *Revitalizing American Industry: Lessons from Our Competitors*, ed. Milton Hochmuth and William Davidson (Cambridge, Mass.: Ballinger Press, 1985), p. 8.

64. Anthony Harrigan, "The American Economy and the National Interest," *Vital Speeches*, vol. lii, no. 13 (April 15, 1986), pp. 399-400.

65. Ibid., p. 400.

66. Ibid.

67. Grant, p. 90.

68. *Businessweek*, March 3, 1986, p. 61.

69. Ichiro Hattori, "Trade Conflicts: A Japanese View," *Vital Speeches*, vol. lii, no. 7 (January 15, 1986), p. 219.

70. Ibid.

71. Ibid.

72. Vernon, pp. 18–19.

73. Cohen and Zysman, p. 60.

74. *Businessweek*, March 3, 1986, p. 60.

75. Ibid., p. 62.

76. Cohen and Zysman, p. 59.

77. Bergstein, "The Trade Deficit Could Be Ruinous'', p. 105.

78. Stephen Kindel, "The Falling Dollar," *Financial World*, vol. clv, no. 9 (April 29, 1986), p. 20.

79. Steven K. Beckner, "The Boom That Won't Quit," *Nation's Business*, vol. lxxiv, no. 4 (April 1986), p. 27.

80. *Conference Board Research Bulletin*, no. 198 (1986), p. 5.

81. Beckner, p. 27.

82. H. Erich Heinemann, "Why Not Have a Service Economy?" *Dun's Business Month*, vol. cxxv, no. 4 (April 1985), p. 64.

83. Roger W. Schmenner, "How Can Service Businesses Survive and Prosper?" *Sloan Management Review*, vol. xxvii, no. 3 (Spring 1986), p. 21.

84. Heinemann, p. 68.

85. *Businessweek*, March 3, 1986, p. 78.

86. Edward N. Wolff, "Industrial Composition, Interindustry Effects and the U.S. Productivity Slowdown," *The Review of Economics and Statistics*, vol. lxvii, no. 2 (May 1985) p. 268.

87. *Businessweek*, March 3, 1986, p. 78.
88. Heinemann, p. 65.
89. *Businessweek*, March 3, 1986, p. 81.
90. Henry Eason, "Keeping the Trade Deficit in the Right Perspective," *Nation's Business*, vol. lxxii, no. 10 (October 1984), p. 56.
91. *Businessweek*, March 2, 1986, p. 81.
92. Ibid., p. 79.
93. George Cabot Lodge and William C. Crom, "U.S. Competitiveness: The Policy Tangle," *Harvard Business Review*, vol. lxiii, no. 1 (November–December 1985), p. 34.
94. John D. A. Cuddy, "Some Reflections on Growth in OECD Economies," *Trade and Development*, no. 6 (1985), p. 49.
95. *New York Times*, August 17, 1986, p. F-3.
96. N. T. Wang, "Penetrating New Markets," *Academy of Political Science of New York City Proceedings*, vol. xxxvi, no. 1 (1986), p. 162.
97. Lawrence and Litan, p. 5.
98. *Businessweek*, April 7, 1986, p. 24.
99. Marotta, p. 236.
100. Weidenbaum, "Freeing Trade", p. 96.

4

POLICY RESPONSES

The current trade policy of the U.S. government differs sharply from the alternative programs advocated respectively by the monetarists and structuralists as means for addressing the American trade deficit. The actual foreign trade policy presently being pursued by the government can be divided into three dimensions. There is, first, a domestic aspect comprised of actions taken or proposed on a purely unilateral basis by various decision-makers in the United States. Second, there is a multilateral element consisting of American participation in joint efforts by groups of major trading nations to regulate and reform the practice of international commerce. Finally, there is a bilateral facet encompassing trade issues, conflicts, and negotiations between the United States and its individual trading partners.

Following World War II, the United States had both an ideological commitment to, and a vested interest in, the liberalization of world trade. Aside from its free market heritage, America had emerged from the war with its economic structure unscathed, its industrial might fully developed, and its advantages over potential trade rivals seemingly insurmountable. Quite naturally, the United States championed the cause of free and open global trade through word and example. Between 1945 and 1975, by itself and in concert with others, America cut its import tar-

iffs to one-tenth of the prohibitively high level set in the early
1930s by the Smoot-Hawley Act.[1] In complementary fashion, the
federal government's stance toward the country's export enterprises was one of benign neglect, resting on an abiding faith in
their huge capital and technological advantages to carry the day
without policy intervention. Indeed, throughout the 1970s, the
nation's external sector was treated by the government as more
of a policy instrument than a proper object of policy. Trade performance per se was subordinated to a variety of international
geopolitical goals, like President Jimmy Carter's limitations on
commercial ties with foreign regimes violating the principles of
his human rights crusade.

The election of Ronald Reagan to the presidency virtually en-
sured the continuance of America's laissez-faire trade policy.
Reagan's inherent conservativism admitted no legitimate role for
government in the area of international trade other than affirmative actions to further liberalize the world's trading system.[2]
As the United States posted ever larger trade deficits, Reagan
appeared oblivious to the nation's growing trade problem in the
eyes of his critics. His apparent disregard for America's worsening trade performance was tellingly demonstrated by an inci-
dent which occurred in the spring of 1985. In April of that year,
Reagan had appointed then–U.S. Trade Representative William
Brock to the post of Secretary of Labor. It was not until June,
however, that the White House submitted the name of Brock's
successor to Congress for confirmation. This episode solidified
what was becoming a general opinion about the Reagan administration's trade policy as expressed by a spokesman for the National Association of Manufacturers in his statement: "We have
a President and an Administration with no straight mind on
trade."[3]

What did his critics expect the president to do in response to
the nation's growing trade imbalance? For many, the expecta-
tion was that Reagan would aggressively use his powers under
the Trade Act of 1974. Section 301 of this act authorizes the
president to initiate investigations by, and consider the findings
of, the Trade Representative concerning "any act, policy or
practice of a foreign government" suspected of violating any international agreement or of being "unjustifiable, unreasonable or

discriminatory and which burdens or restricts United States commerce."[4] Should these hearings result in a positive finding, the president is empowered to call for negotiations with the government in question, and if a satisfactory resolution cannot be reached, he has the prerogative of imposing a range of retaliatory measures—tariff hikes, reduced quotas, etc.—on imports from that nation. In sections 201 through 203, the president is granted discretionary power to assist American domestic producers damaged by foreign competition once they have demonstrated current or prospective harm to the International Trade Commission. This relief can be extended for a period of up to five years and may be issued regardless of whether the damage is linked to an unfair trade practice by a foreign state.[5]

Given their presumption that unfair foreign trade policies had caused extensive damage to America's export and import-competing businesses, it was understandable that the administration's detractors should berate the president for failing to make use of these weapons. In truth, the administration had responded to charges of both unfair trade practices and petitions from suffering domestic industries on a number of occasions. Admittedly, Reagan had rarely resorted to transparent import restrictions in these instances. Instead, he had negotiated several Voluntary Restraint Agreements to curb the flow of imports from countries enjoying large sectoral/industry-wide surpluses against the United States.[6] During the 1980s, these orderly marketing arrangements had been imposed on a range of imports including automobiles, steel, clothing, and meat.[7] In 1981, nontariff import controls protected 20 percent of domestic manufacturers. By 1986, 35 percent were being relieved of foreign competition through quota and quotalike devices.[8] Since they were established with consent of the affected trade partner, they offered the advantage of concealing any overt protectionist intent. For a time, then, the Reagan administration had found a way of placating the demands of politically powerful domestic producers without seeming to violate its own free trade rhetoric.

Paradoxically, it was the impression of trade complacency which the administration projected, rather than the actual substance of its policies, which caused Congress to pit itself against the executive by demanding sterner action. Having delegated a portion of its powers over foreign trade to the president in the 1974 act, the legislature set about to reclaim its constitutional authority to regulate commerce with foreign nations.[9] The opening salvo of this campaign was fired in March 1985, when the Senate passed a resolution calling for retaliatory action against Japan by a vote of ninety-two to zero.[10] Congress had periodically made protectionist noises throughout the 1970s, but, as I. M. Destler sees it, prior to 1985, its aim was *not* to carry through on these cries. Rather, it was simply to appear tough on foreign trade issues in the minds of their constituents that senators and representatives had pushed for protectionist measures, never meaning for them to be implemented. However, since President Reagan appeared blithely unconcerned about the impact of foreign trade on America's industries and regions, Congress became increasingly preoccupied with divorcing itself from a "do nothing" president in the public's view. Because "the Administration was not providing members of Congress with political help and political insulation at a time when they needed it more than ever," Destler writes, "the number of bills soared"[11] as both Democrats and Republicans were caught up in a protectionist drive that they did not initially want.

The textile bill of 1985 represented the first broad piece of legislation daring the president to harden his stance on trade or take the political heat for continued passivity. This bill would have rolled back textile imports from Hong Kong, Taiwan, and South Korea by 30 percent and frozen textile shipments from nine other developing countries at their 1984 quota levels. Endorsed by both houses in the summer of 1985, the textile bill was vetoed by the president in December of that year. Ultimately, it was only by working furiously to reach new textile quotas with Hong Kong, Taiwan, and South Korea in the summer of 1986 that Reagan was able to avert a congressional override of his veto.[12] Although the textile bill was a tactical defeat for protectionists within Congress, it performed the strategic function of prodding the president to adopt a far more active stance on foreign trade in general.[13]

On September 23, 1985 (immediately following the passage of the textile bill), the president announced a major policy shift from noninterventionism to selective intervention on behalf of free *and* fair trade. Proclaiming "We're going after unfair trade practices more aggressively than any previous Administration,"[14] Reagan enumerated a series of steps directed at America's trade competitors. Most significantly, instead of waiting for complaints from the private sector, the president committed his office to originating section 301 investigations on its own initiative.[15] He immediately made good on this promise, setting in motion cases against Brazil's restrictions on American computer imports[16] and South Korea's lack of statutory protection against piracy of American intellectual property[17] among others. In addition, following suggestions made by Commerce Secretary Malcolm Baldridge, Reagan submitted a series of bills to Congress relaxing antitrust standards for industries distressed by foreign competition.[18]

The largest and most expensive trade-related program inaugurated by the federal government in 1985 was not a trade measure per se, but a vast expansion of the nation's agricultural support system. Enthusiastically signed by the president in December 1985, the new farm bill established a much more extensive web of agricultural export subsidies and credits to America's farmers than ever before. Most importantly, the pricing mechanism for subsidized farm exports was completely revised, allowing the country's agricultural producers to offer their goods in foreign markets at prices below the cost of production and still realize a profit. Ironically, the new arrangement essentially duplicated that of European Economic Community's farm export program, the latter being an "unfair" trade policy which the Reagan administration had consistently characterized as a senseless dumping of food lacking any economic justification. Touted as "the most aggressive export program" in U.S. history, the new farm relief package is also the most costly, with annual government expenditures projected at between $25 billion and $35 billion.[19]

From September 1985 through the summer of the following year, Reagan and his newly appointed Trade Representative Clayton Yeutter stepped up their use of retaliatory threats to negotiate a wide spectrum of bilateral and multilateral trade balancing measures, some aimed at lowering foreign tariff/nontariff barriers, others at countering foreign export subsidies, still others at curbing imports via quotas. In part, this campaign was motivated by the president's awareness of foreign trade as an emerging political issue at large, but, at bottom, it was basically a defensive tactic designed to limit congressional support for stronger protectionist action.[20]

Although the textile bill had been defeated, an even greater challenge to Reagan's moderate policies was brewing in Congress. In the summer of 1985, a protectionist coalition led by Representatives Dan Rostenkowski and Richard Gephart along with Senator Lloyd Bensten sponsored the Trade Emergency and Export Promotion Act of 1985.[21] This bill called for an automatic 25 percent tariff surcharge on goods imported from countries running large trade surpluses with the United States, including Japan, South Korea, Taiwan, and Brazil.[22] The act stalled, but a diluted version of its central provision found its way into an Omnibus Foreign Trade Bill subsequently proposed by Senator John Danforth. The two chief features of the Danforth piece were addressed to the supposed shortcomings of the 1974 Trade Act. The first, modifying section 301, *required* the president to take retaliatory action against a foreign nation that achieves an "excessive" trade surplus with the United States through unfair trade practices and then fails to negotiate a 10 percent annual reduction in that surplus. The second, altering sections 201 through 203, calls for immediate relief of domestic industries found to have been injured by foreign trade by the International Trade Commission *without* presidential review of the case.[23] The common ingredient in both these clauses is their elimination of presidential discretion in applying trade repraisals against foreign competitors and granting relief to domestic producers.[24] Castigated by Reagan as "Kamikaze legislation," this "anti-trade bill"[25] was approved by the House of Representatives in May 1986 by a vote of 295 to 115.[26] Although the bill did not reach a vote in the Senate in 1986, a version of it is likely to receive passage by the upper house in 1987.

Reviewing the unilateral dimension of current U.S. trade policy, three points are evident. First, as embodied in the ongoing conflict between Congress and the president, there is no consensus within the federal government about how America should respond to its declining trade performance. In the absense of a coherent strategy for handling the trade problem, sound economic reasoning has been pushed aside by narrow political calculation. Second, the general drift of American trade policy has been toward increased protectionism. Congress has made it clear that it will accommodate the protectionist demands of domestic producers, while the president has attempted to dampen the surge by applying his own brand of selective protectionism. Third, the most substantial piece of legislation endorsed by the legislature and the executive, the new farm bill, is an enormously expensive measure of dubious effectiveness. By increasing federal government expenditures some $25 billion to $35 billion a year above prior farm support programs, the new agricultural export act adds to the same internal disequilibrium which has spilled over into the nation's external accounts.

The United States is signatory to (and a cofounder of) the General Agreement on Tariffs and Trade (GATT). Covering four-fifths of the total value of world trade by its ninety-two members, the GATT is the most prominent part of America's multilateral trade policy dimension. The GATT arose after World War II as an interim device for promoting free global trade until a permanent International Trade Organization (ITO) could be established. For a variety of reasons, the ITO never saw the light of day; hence, the GATT itself was institutionalized with its Geneva headquarters supervising "rounds" of negotiating sessions.[27] With each round requiring five to six years of deliberations, thus far a total of seven have been completed, the last two being the Sixth or Kennedy Round (1962–1967) and the Seventh or Tokyo Round (1973–1979).[28] From the standpoint of tariff reductions on merchandise imports, the GATT has proven an eminent success, cutting average tariff rates worldwide from a prevailing 40 percent after World War II to a mere 5 percent in 1986.[29] However, even as transparent trade restrictions were dismantled, nontariff barriers sprang up to take their place.[30] Hence, during the Tokyo Round, various types of nontariff barriers dominated the agenda, amendments were passed to prohibit or limit their use, and a dispute resolution procedure was put in place for handling complaints about them.[31]

On the eve of the Eighth or Uruguay Round, a host of problems beset the GATT. First and foremost, the GATT is an extremely weak agency, lacking effective enforcement powers.[32] Its real force resides in sanctions or threats of sanctions applied by its individual members against other GATT participants alleged to be in violation of its rules. Second, as exemplified in America's Voluntary Export Restraints, the substitution of nontariff for tariff barriers is now widespread. National governments have displayed an inexhaustible capacity to construct ever more subtle NTBs.[33] Consequently, while blatant NTBs have been covered under the GATT, its supervisors are perpetually confronted with novel schemes for discriminating against foreign goods as part of a moving target syndrome. Third, outside of manufactured goods, GATT is severely limited. On the whole, international commerce in agriculture and services, protection of intellectual property, and treatment of direct investment do not enjoy detailed coverage under GATT. Lastly, as GATT membership has grown from twenty-two to nearly one hundred nations, fairly rigid blocs have emerged within it. The most serious of these schisms is that between the industrial countries and the developing nations of the Third World. Both groups have successfully erected ancillary devices within the GATT framework on behalf of their respective interests. On the one hand, between 1971 and 1976, the developing countries pushed for preferential treatment of their manufactured exports through General Systems of Preferences (GSPs). Granted on a bilateral basis by industrialized nations to select developing economies, these preferences are allowed as an exception to the GATT which undermines its broader nondiscriminatory spirit. On the other hand, the United States and other developed nations erected orderly marketing arrangements under the GATT umbrella to limit competition from developing country commodity imports. The most notorious of these is the Multi-Fiber Agreement (MFA), which has been successively renewed since the early 1960s to curb textile/clothing exports from the Third World to developed nations via a network of negotiated quotas.[34] In fact, this trade distorting system is based on a single, multilateral agreement administered by the GATT's own Textile Committee. In essence, both GSPs and the MFA undercut the GATT's overall purpose of eliminating artificial barriers to trade, but both are legitimized within the GATT as exceptions, while the latter operates through the GATT itself.

When the world's trading nations sat down to the opening talks of the Uruguay Round in mid-September 1986, all of these problems plagued negotiations. Prior to the initial sessions, the United States warned its GATT partners that unless priority was given to matters affecting America's trade interests, particularly trade liberalization in agriculture and services, it would withdraw from the talks.[35]

America found itself squarely at odds with the European community nations on the issue of agricultural subsidies, the Europeans refusing a major cutback in their farm support programs despite American pressure. The United States was upstaged on this front, however. A coalition of fourteen major agricultural exporters headed by Australia, Argentina, and Canada sought complete elimination of all government agricultural support programs and all import barriers to farm products. As to the liberalization of service transactions and greater protection for intellectual property, a group of developing nations led by Brazil and India strongly opposed extension of GATT provisions to these fields, arguing that their own "infant" service industries would be overwhelmed by competition from advanced, service-exporting economies. At the same time, Third World representatives sought to retain their privileges under GSPs and phase out the MFA, while the developed nations wanted to reduce GSPs and keep the MFA in full force.

Under the direction of Trade Representative Yeutter, the American delegation achieved nearly all of its preconditions in the first sessions of the Uruguay Round.[36] However, as Robert Lawrence observes, even under the fast track approach adopted by the conferees at the behest of the United States, it will require at least four years for Eight Round negotiations to be completed and several more years before liberalizations are put into operation.[37] Add to this necessary delay the GATT's lack of enforcement power and its vulnerability to subtle NTBs, and the degree of progress which can be made through the Uruguay Round appears decidedly circumscribed.

Although the GATT covers a broad and growing range of matters related directly to trade policies, it does not deal with those fundamental macroeconomic forces which exert such a strong influence over international trade patterns, most notably relative currency values and growth rate differentials. As the U.S. trade record continued to erode, the Reagan administration began to have second thoughts about the strength of the dollar. Starting in March 1985, American monetary authorities sought to improve the nation's trade performance by intervening in exchange markets to drive the dollar down.[38] They fully realized, however, that they could not affect the dollar's value to any appreciable extent without the cooperation of other major trading nations.

On September 22, 1985, one day before the president's fair trade program was announced, Treasury Secretary James Baker met with finance ministers and central bankers from Japan, West Germany, France, and Britain at New York City's Plaza Hotel. The assembled officials agreed that the magnitude of the American trade deficit was a danger to world commerce as a whole and that coordinated action was necessary to weaken the dollar. The Plaza conclave issued a joint declaration calling for "some further orderly appreciation of the main non-dollar currencies against the dollar"[39] and announcing the participants' resolve to take steps toward that end. In late September and early October, central banks from the five exchanged some $10.2 billion in dollars for other currencies,[40] with the Bank of Japan selling $3 billion in dollars for a like amount of yen in just two days.[41] In itself, this effort was still too small to impact upon relative exchange values given the enormous volume of forex trading in currency markets around the globe. Nonetheless, by signaling their unified intention to reduce the dollar's value, the Plaza conferees sent a message to currency traders which the latter heeded by swapping a portion of their dollar holdings for yen, marks, francs, and pounds. The intended outcome was achieved with the understanding that accelerated dollar depreciation would assist the United States in moving its trade and current accounts toward balance.

Hailed as a milestone event in America's drive to upgrade its international competitiveness, the Plaza Accord did not attain a second goal sought by the United States. Secretary Baker had hoped to persuade the Japanese and West Germans to adopt more expansionary fiscal policies as means for pushing their currencies up against the dollar and increasing demand for American goods in their home markets.[42] It was at the Tokyo Summit of

May 1986 that this second approach to redressing the American trade imbalance was broached again. The Tokyo Summit brought together the heads of the G-5 Plaza meeting nations along with the prime ministers of Canada and Italy as the Group of Five was expanded into a Group of Seven. The new body was charged with (1) working to coordinate the domestic economic policies of their respective countries for the purpose of reducing their external imbalances (deficits and surpluses alike) and (2) managing exchange rate movements in order to reduce rate volatility and keep individual currencies in line with actual economic performance. The meeting appeared to have historic importance as the first instance of formal coordination in the macroeconomic policies of the major powers and in shifting the world's exchange rate regime away from a free floating arrangement and toward a managed floating system.[43]

During the summer of 1986, the sense of common purpose which had characterized the Plaza and Tokyo meetings evaporated as acrimonious disputes over exchange rates and domestic policies erupted.[44] In March 1986 West German and Japanese monetary officials instituted discount rate cuts in their economies in coordination with a Federal Reserve Board discount rate reduction. A month later, West Germany refused to remain in step, as only Japan and the United States issued another discount rate cut, and in July and August, unable to persuade the Japanese to follow its lead, the Fed was forced to go it alone in carrying out two further reductions.[45] Indeed, by September 1986, twelve European nations banded together to intervene in currency markets for the purpose of pushing the dollar *up* against the West German mark.[46]

The refusal of other industrial powers to go along with America on this front was grounded in two considerations and one basic criticism. First, since their individual currencies had already appreciated so sharply against the dollar, Japan and West Germany saw no justification for a further movement in this direction given the negative impact it was already having on their export volumes. Second, the United States' insistence that its Japanese and West European trade partners adopt expansionary monetary and fiscal policies ran directly counter to the long-term interest of these nations in keeping domestic price inflation un-

der control. Most importantly, these governments argued vigor-
ously that the United States was failing to live up to its end of
the Tokyo Summit bargain. Specifically, the federal government
had done nothing to reduce its budget deficit in the months following the Tokyo sessions. Why, then, should Japan and West
Germany take actions to help the United States with its external
imbalance at costs and risks to themselves when America was
not taking the most essential step to help itself?

It is unlikely that actions taken by the U.S. government through
multilateral channels will lead to any significant improvement in
America's trade performance. Despite its flaws, the GATT remains the world's central institutional mechanism for establishing, maintaining, and clarifying norms of international commerce. As such, it clearly deserves the continued support of the
United States. Yet its weaknessess are many, and even assuming that foreign trade practices are a major cause of America's
trade deficits, relying on GATT to redress them is simply un-
realistic. Policy coordination and joint exchange rate management are fine on paper, but, in practice, different nations have
divergent and frequently conflicting objectives. Consequently, the
Tokyo Summit approach to America's external imbalance could
not be sustained. In all fairness, calling on others to play a prime
role in remedying America's foreign trade problems by voluntarily reducing their own competitiveness and risking domestic price
instability is asking far too much.

The bilateral dimension of current American trade policy re-
volves around negotiated settlements of trade conflicts between
the United States and other nations, along with efforts to culti-
vate open and equitable two-way trade. Since the outset of the
1980s, American trade officials have applied strong pressures on
their Japanese counterparts to open their nation's markets to U.S.
exports and to eliminate policies which lend Japanese products
an unfair edge in American and third-country markets. In the
first years of the decade, the United States was able to make
formal headway on both these counts, with, for example, Japan
promising to phase out the closed procurement system of the
quasipublic Nippon Telegraph and Telephone company[47] and
voluntarily limiting its exports of automobiles and steel to the
United States.[48]

As to the opening of its markets through the removal of non-tariff barriers, American exporters have been sorely disappointed with the results, complaining that the Japanese have not followed through on their promises in any meaningful sense. By contrast, even when voluntary export quotas on Japanese auto exports to the United States were lifted in April 1985, Japanese producers continued to follow them on an informal basis. It was not their wish to contribute to a balanced U.S.–Japan trade account that motivated them, however, but their desire to continue receiving large profit margins on their sales to the United States.[49]

Disgusted with Japan's failure to match words with deeds, the U.S. Senate passed its March 1985 nonbinding resolution directing the president to enforce existing treaty obligations with Japan and threaten retaliatory action against unfair Japanese trade policies.[50] In his talks with Japanese Prime Minister Yasuhiro Nakasone a month later, Reagan did not explicitly threaten trade reprisals, but he did target four product groups (lumber, pharmaceuticals/medical equipment, sophisticated electronics, and telecommunications) for action. The president argued that in each of these areas, while American manufacturers held a clear-cut competitive edge over the Japanese, their shares of Japanese markets were abnormally small. On April 9, 1985, Nakasone responded. Appearing on Japanese television, he exhorted his countrymen to "buy American," announced tariff reductions on some 1800 items and proclaimed that United States access to Japanese markets should be free, "with any restrictions as exceptions."[51]

In 1986, two bitter trade disputes were added to the list of commercial conflicts between America and Japan. The first involved charges that Japanese nontariff barriers were unduly restricting sales of American-made computer chips and that Japanese chip makers were dumping their goods in world markets at prices well below their cost of production. In July 1986, a settlement of sorts was reached as the United States threatened to impose stiff antidumping duties on Japanese semiconductors shipped to America. Under the agreement, Japan pledged to assist American chip manufacturers in expanding their share of the Japanese market from 8.5 percent in 1986 to a target of 20 percent by 1991, and MITI took on the uncharacteristic role of

monitoring the prices of Japanese semiconductor exports and
clamping down on dumping.[52] The settlement, however, was met
with skepticism by the American semiconductor industry. Industry spokesmen noted that in 1984, the Japanese government
had signed two pacts almost identical to the 1986 settlement, but
this did not translate into increased American sales in Japan or
deter private Japanese producers from dumping their chips.[53] Thus
far, the Japanese have boosted their price on chips sold in the
United States, but they have already been charged with continuing to dump chips in third country markets.[54]

The second major trade row between America and Japan to
emerge in 1986 concerned construction of a new $8 billion air-
port in Osaka Bay by the Japanese parastatal Kansai International Airport Company (KIAC). When KIAC failed to consider
bids from American construction firms, they complained bitterly. Construction is an area of comparative advantage for the
United States relative to Japan, and with some $60 billion in
bridges, airports, and other infrastructural projects scheduled for
completion in Japan over the next twenty years, there exists a
strong potential for increased service exports from the United
States in this field. Progress on resolving the Osaka Airport tiff
does not bode well for the realization of this opportunity. Despite Prime Minister Nakasone's personal intervention in the af-
fair, KIAC managers have refused to alter their procurement
policies.[55] On the whole, U.S.–Japan bilateral trade negotiations
have been marred by accusations that the Japanese are not bargaining in good faith, and limited by the Japanese government's
inability to dismantle deeply rooted nontariff barriers and unfair
practices by private and semipublic bodies. Hence, despite the
warmth of the "Ron-Yasu" relationship, a strong element of dis-
trust now darkens the future course of trade negotiations between the two countries.

In sharp relief to Japanese-American trade relations, bilateral
negotiations between the United States and Canada have been
characterized by a frank, above-board quality. More than two
decades ago, the United States and Canada ironed out a long-
standing dispute over two-way trade in automobiles, allowing
the value of this flow to jump from $735 million in 1964 to $46
billion in 1984.[56] This was the start of a continuing process of

trade liberalization under which 80 percent of Canadian exports to the United States and 65 percent of American exports to Canada were scheduled for duty-free treatment by 1987.[57] Once the nationalistic Prime Minister Pierre Trudeau had been replaced by Brian Mulroney, the outlook for even more progress brightened. In fact, at the start of 1986, American and Canadian trade negotiators were awaiting the commencement of talks for the establishment of a Free Trade Area (FTA) featuring completely unimpeded movement of all items crossing the Canadian-American border.[58]

As 1986 began, the initiation of Free Trade Area talks between the United States at Canada by year's end appeared to be a virtual certainty. In the spring, however, a comparatively minor dispute concerning Canadian lumber exports to America put the future of the FTA in grave doubt. U.S. timber producers charged that Canada's provincial governments were unfairly subsidizing their lumber manufacturers by allowing them to harvest trees from public lands without charging a "stumpage" fee reflecting their fair market value.[59] The U.S. International Trade Commission had heard this complaint in 1985 and had rejected the American lumber industry's claims, but in April 1986 the Senate Finance Committee, headed by Oregon Senator Robert Packwood, took up the complaint and asked President Reagan to delay FTA negotiations until a settlement could be reached.[60] As it turns out, Reagan went even further. In May, he imposed a stunning 35 percent import surcharge on Canadian exports of cedar shakes and shingles. Understandably miffed, the Mulroney government reacted by raising existing tariffs and restoring old ones on a wide range of American goods, including books, computer parts, tea, oats, and asphalt. The real shame of the so-called Shingle War was that the Canadian products in question amounted to less than one-seventh of 1 percent of U.S.–Canadian trade by volume,[61] yet they were at the center of an overblown maelstrom which had temporarily derailed the creation of a comprehensive Free Trade Area. More sinned against than sinning, the Canadians have ample reason to complain about the interference of narrow political interests in what was previously a harmonious trade relation.

Trade relations between the United States and the nations of

the E.E.C. resemble those of America and Canada in their can-
dor and those of America and Japan in their obduracy. After
World War II, the United States was highly instrumental in rebuilding the ravaged economics of Western Europe and in the
very formation of the E.E.C. The principal motive behind these
policies was America's interest in the development of a large,
secure, and unified market for its exports. Thus, for a time, the
United States tolerated the high external tariffs and extensive
subsidies of the fledgling E.E.C. as a necessary cost of achieving
this broader goal.[62] During the last half of the 1960s, however,
what was to become the chief source of conflict between the
United States and Europe appeared in the form of the Common
Agricultural Policy.[63] Not only did the CAP increase tariff barriers against American exports to Europe, it also provided the
community's farmers with a means of increasing their price
competitiveness against American agricultural exports at home
and in third country markets. Enjoying a privileged status within
the E.E.C. the CAP has progressively diminished the importance of Europe to the United States as an export outlet and
transformed the overall trade relationship between the two into
one of fierce competition. Although other European trade and
industrial policies have generated sharp frictions, particularly
subsidies granted by individual European governments to their
steel manufacturers, it is the CAP which has been the main bone
of contention in U.S.–E.E.C. trade relations for the past twenty
years.

    In the mid-1980s, intense conflicts over agriculture and, to a
lesser extent, steel, caused a marked deterioration in America's
trade relations with Western Europe. The entrance of Spain and
Portugal into the community meant the extension of the CAP
system to these economies, and, with it, lost export sales for the
United States.[64] The E.E.C.'s policy of favoring citrus exports
from non-E.E.C. Mediterranean sources over American products was another prominent source of trade hostility in 1985 and
1986, as were American quotas on imports of subsidized European steel. As each of these issues surfaced in rapid succession,
both sides reacted with tariff hikes and it appeared that a full-
blown trade war was imminent. Fortunately, reason prevailed.
After the declaration of a six month truce in July 1986,[65] Amer-

ican and E.E.C. trade negotiators were able to reach agreements on all of these matters.[66] Even though an escalation of nascent trade war was averted for the time being, similar disputes are likely to flare up in the immediate future because neither side has shown any sign of altering its stance on agricultural export supports. Indeed, by expanding its own farm subsidy system to match the CPA's, the United States has implicitly declared its intention to go head-to-head with the Europeans in competing for shares of global agricultural markets.

Since the volume of trade flows between the United States and the nations of the Third World was relatively small prior to 1980, the conflicts which now plague trade relations between America and the developing nations are of comparatively recent vintage. Following the proclamation of President Reagan's fair trade program, the United States took a very aggressive posture in its bilateral trade negotiations with trade surplus developing countries, especially the newly industrialized lands of East Asia. Warning of stern retaliatory measures, American trade officials compelled South Korea, Taiwan, and Hong Kong to reduce their import tariff rates, to open their markets to American service exports, to provide greater protection for American-owned intellectual property,[67] and, within the framework of the MFA, to limit growth in their shipments of textiles/clothing to the United States.[68]

On the other side of the coin, America has been far less successful in its drive to force open Latin American markets to its exports. Perhaps the most heated dispute between the United States and Latin America concerns America's protests against Brazil's Informatics Law. Enacted in 1984, the Informatics Law imposes a complete ban on imports of foreign-made computers and computer-related items, and, given America's interest in high-tech exports, the law has been a thorn to the United States since its passage. Indeed, Brazil's computer-import ban was the first target of President Reagan's section 301 investigations as a clear-cut example of unfair foreign trade practices in action. In contrast to the swift response brought about by sanction threats toward East Asian nations, the Brazilian government has steadfastly rejected any change in its policy of blanket protection for its domestic computer industry. During a September 1986 meeting between President Reagan and Brazilian President Jose Sarney, Reagan took the unusual step of directly cautioning Sarney on this matter, but the latter refused to budge.[69]

Looking back on the collective record of American efforts to improve the nation's trade performance through bilateral negotiations, the results yielded to date have been mixed, but generally disappointing. Where the United States has a strong case and the necessary leverage to effect change—in the cases of South Korea, Taiwan, and Hong Kong—some progress has been made. But in its dealings with more powerful trade competitors, Japan and the E.E.C., for example, the United States has not begun to bridge its long-standing differences with these governments and the prospects for their resolution in the near term are slim. Indeed, for America's trade relations with Canada, the fair trade program appears to have done more harm than good.

All in all, the conduct of American foreign trade policy along unilateral, bilateral, and multilateral lines has suffered from a single underlying defect. In all of these spheres, the American government has proceeded under the assumption that the country's growing trade deficit is primarily the outcome of forces and policies stemming from abroad. Part of this denial is clearly motivated by the desire of elected officials to exonerate themselves for America's worsening trade performance, and, in this sense, understandable. Far more troubling, however, it seems as if these same officials are beginning to believe in their own rhetoric. Whatever their motive, taking a shallow and false premise as the starting point for formulating a response to the nation's trade imbalance precludes effective action. In fact, as we shall discover in the remainder of this chapter, the United States has not taken the requisite action to put its macroeconomic house in order as advocated by the monetarists, nor has it taken seriously the potential for enhancing its international competitiveness through a comprehensive industrial policy as proposed by the structuralists.

THE MONETARIST POSITION

The essence of the monetarist approach for moving America's trade and current accounts toward equilibrium is the repression of aggregate domestic demand. Through the conjunction of tightened fiscal and monetary policies, internal public and private consumption can be brought into line with the actual value of national output. As this occurs, the dollar will fall in value relative to the currencies of our major trading partners since the contraction of the American economy will reduce its attractiveness as an investment vehicle in global exchange markets. The depreciation of the dollar, in turn, will assist export and import-competing enterprises in regaining price competitiveness in markets around the world. Simultaneously, America's productive resources will gradually shift from domestic- to export-oriented activities as private entrepreneurs search for greater demand than is present in their home markets.

Before examining the specifics of the monetarist policy response to the trade deficit, two points concerning its overall thrust should be highlighted. First, it is somewhat misleading to think of the monetarist prescription as consisting of policy measures in a constructive sense. The monetarists' bottom line is that, in the long run, each country must match its domestic absorption expenditures to productive capacity,[70] and that any tinkering with the economy by the government to alter the relationship is ultimately self-defeating. Indeed, interference with natural market mechanisms, particularly an artificially stimulative fiscal policy and an accommodationist expansion of the money supply, is the proximate cause of America's trade ills since it permitted the nation to live beyond its means. For the monetarists, adopting more austere fiscal and monetary regimes is not so much a matter of redirecting policy as it is a matter of conforming to the dictates of underlying economic conditions. Without meaning to split hairs, it is not that the federal government should now counterbalance past expansionism with contractionism, it is that the federal government ought never have allowed its policies to deviate from those warranted by basic macroeconomic circumstances in the first place.

Second, the initial impact of the monetarist belt-tightening course for dealing with the trade deficit will be to *reinforce* the two chief effects of the trade imbalance upon the American economy, that is, a growth slowdown accompanied by a temporary spurt in inflation. Cutting away the external props that have supported the nation's economy during the 1980s, that is, cheap foreign imports and an inflow of capital from abroad, will at first hasten the coming of the stagflationary effect which our external imbalance is bound to have. Once this syndrome has been allowed to run its natural, cyclical course, and balance has been achieved at a lower level of demand, then, and only then, will America be able to shake off the consequences of the trade deficit on a lasting basis.

The cornerstone of the monetarist response to the trade problem is the sharp and immediate reduction of the Federal Government's yearly budget deficits. From the monetarist perspective, the government's books must be brought under control by slashing public sector expenditures.[71] As former Federal Reserve Board member Preston Martin testified before a congressional committee, "Progress in controlling the spending side of the budget is vital"[72] for correcting the nation's trade and current accounts, since the only alternative would be to increase revenues through taxes and impose yet another burden on the workings of the private sector. The necessity of addressing runaway federal government spending has been recognized by both public and private analysts of current U.S. trade performance. "There are three things that can be done to deal with the trade problem," according to Bell & Howell Chairman Donald Frey, "deficit reduction, deficit reduction, deficit reduction."[73] Achieving a closer correspondence between the government's income and outlays would obviate the need for imported foreign capital, and, with it, superfluous purchases of foreign goods and services. Domestic interest rates would eventually decline as the public sector's demand for additional credit is curbed, and this would permit increased private sector investment "to upgrade productive facilities and further improve the competitiveness of U.S. industries."[74] As we shall soon discover, in the course espoused by the monetarists, fiscal and monetary discipline go hand-in-hand: Without significant progress in cutting federal expenditures, the necessary return to a prudent monetary policy will result in skyrocketing interest rates and a much deeper recession than that preordained by the strictures of trade-related adjustment.

During the fall of 1985, the U.S. Congress ratified, and President Reagan signed, the Balanced Budget and Emergency Deficit Control Act, known colloquially as the Gramm-Rudman

Amendment. Using 1985's $212 billion federal budget deficit as a benchmark, Gramm-Rudman targeted a reduction in fiscal shortfalls from a maximum deficit of $208 billion in 1986 to complete balance by 1991. The act required Congress to either present the president with successive annual budgets conforming to these ceilings or subject all federally funded programs to proportionate and automatic cuts mandated by an independent government agency.[75] In July 1986, the U.S. Supreme Court struck down the Gramm-Rudman mechanism as a violation of the constitutional doctrine of the separation of powers, but a revised method of applying across-the-board spending reductions is now being prepared, and, in the opinion of many, Gramm-Rudman II will comply with constitutional standards.[76] Orthodox monetarists are by no means thrilled with Gramm-Rudman: Its mechanical caste violates the free-choice premises of rational economic decision-making cherished by them. Nevertheless, since Congress and the president remain at loggerheads over what types of federal programs should bear the brunt of the deficit paring process, this type of involuntary arrangement is tolerated by the monetarists as a necessary evil.

The devaluation of the dollar figures prominently in the monetarist program for restoring the price competitiveness of American wares.[77] Consequently, one might conclude that actions taken to drive the dollar down, as in the Plaza Accord, would receive their unqualified blessing. This, however, is not the case. First and foremost, currency market intervention, like all forms of government interference, is anathema to the monetarists by definition. Second, neither the Plaza Agreement nor President Reagan's fair trade program takes into account the necessity of federal budget deficit reduction.[78] It is through the unimpeded operation of currency markets reacting to rectified conditions within the United States that the dollar should be allowed to seek its proper level, not currency intervention or exchange rate management taken independently of sorely needed changes in America's macroeconomic environment. Along with others, the monetarists point out that there is no firm consensus about a correct exchange rate for the dollar against other currencies[79] because that rate must be set on a fluid basis by markets, as opposed to the rigid calculations of bureaucrats. In fact, well before the Plaza meeting, the top-heavy dollar was dropping from its February 1985 peak against the G-10 currencies through the unfettered workings of the floating rate system.[80] Between the first quarter of 1985 and the third quarter of 1986, the Japanese yen and the German mark appreciated against the dollar respectively by approximately 45 percent and 35 percent, not because the world's central bankers said they should, but because currency market traders recognized that they were undervalued in relation to the dollar.[81] A realistic exchange rate for the national currency is a critical element in the monetarist response to the trade imbalance, but attempting to manage its decline through currency market intervention is not a valid means for its attainment.

If the Plaza Accord contravenes monetarism's insistence on market-based adjustment of the trade deficit, cuts in the Federal Reserve Board's discount rate to weaken the dollar are even more foolhardy from the monetarist standpoint. In less than six months (March 1986 to August 1986), the Fed lowered its discount rate on four separate occasions amounting to a 200 basis point decline in the cost of funds to the nation's banks. Admittedly, these actions had the temporary effect of helping to bring the dollar down by reducing the positive interest rate differential between the United States and its major trading partners.[82] Once again, however, this artificial and imprudent method of realigning currencies does not meet the monetarists' central criteria of fostering long-term stability in the American economy. Within monetarist theory, virtually the only positive function which governments can assume in regulating their domestic economies is to maintain a steady, moderate growth in monetary aggregates to assure a stable level of noninflationary growth. "The overriding task of monetary policy," in the words of Preston Martin, "is to ensure long-run price stability and thereby sustainable long-run economic growth."[83] In the monetarist context, then, the Federal Reserve Board's reliance upon discount rate cuts to bring the dollar down is merely an extension of what must be characterized as a wildly expansionary policy upon the part of the Fed. During 1985, with the Fed pumping money into the economy through a loose, growth-accommodating policy, the nation's cash and short-term deposits (M_1) grew at the unusually fast pace of

12 percent. Given further impetus from discount rate cuts in 1986, monetary growth climbed to a 19 percent annualized rate during the first half of the year.[84] From the monetarist standpoint, having used monetary credit creation as a stimulus to growth in the past, the Fed is now proceeding along the same course under the guise of doing something about the nation's trade deficit.

Particularly when combined with the initially inflationary effect of currency depreciation, the monetarists assert that this inordinately high pace of monetary expansion must ultimately result in increased domestic price inflation. The fact that the monetary stimulus radiating from Fed discount rate reductions has not yet led to an upturn in American inflation rates is something of a puzzle to monetarists. Indeed, the failure of prices to reflect rapid growth in monetary aggregates during the mid-1980s has prompted critics of monetarism to launch a general assault against monetarist theory. Convinced of the validity of the relationship between monetary growth and domestic inflation, the monetarists allude to marginal forces which have been keeping prices in American markets down, especially the sharp decline of energy costs for producers and consumers. In the end, they sternly warn, today's discount rate cuts will inevitably leave their imprint on tomorrow's price tags.

How would the monetarists conduct monetary policy within the context of the American trade deficit? They would undoubtedly seek a change toward tighter monetary/credit conditions by increasing the discount rate. True, in the near term, raising the discount rate would induce foreign investors to bid up the value of the dollar in seeking higher rates of return in the United States and the foreign capital inflow would continue. However, in the long run, drying out credit markets would act to reduce aggregate consumption in general and purchases of imported goods in particular. Moreover, since the monetarist program depends absolutely on a reduction of the federal budget deficit, a portion of the interest rate rise stemming from monetary contraction would be mitigated by a simultaneous decrease in the government's absorption of private savings. In a sense, reversing the thrust of monetary policy by bringing growth of the money supply into a prudent range would have the salutary effect of placing the onus of adjustment where it belongs: on the need for cutting the federal government's deficit expenditures. Monetary policy cannot be used as a way of avoiding the pains of past, present, and future fiscal profligacy by allowing national consumption to outstrip output via debt and inflation. It is only within an environment of stable monetary growth that slashing the federal budget deficit can have a permanent positive influence on America's external accounts.

The monetarists are extremely leery of recent efforts to transfer part of the burden of trade-related adjustment onto the shoulders of our trading partners. A number of officials within government, including ex-International Trade Commission Chairwoman Paula Stern,[85] Secretary of Commerce Malcolm Baldridge,[86] and, most conspicuously, Federal Reserve Board Chairman Paul Volcker,[87] have urged the governments of Japan and West Germany to reduce their external surpluses and allow for increased purchase of American-made imports by adopting more expansionary fiscal and monetary policies. Indeed, Japan, for one, has tried to counter the growth slowdown in its domestic economy brought about by the yen's upward movement (and hence a reduction in export-led growth) through discount rate cuts, supplementary budget appropriations, consumption-favoring tax reforms, and the like.[88] The Germans have been far more circumspect in this regard. They have eschewed reflationary measures, seeing economic growth as adequate, the existing expansion rate of the monetary supply as already too high, discount rate cuts as a precursor to capital flight, and the specter of domestic price inflation lurking in the background.[89] For the monetarists, stimulating import demand through the reflation of the economies of our main trading partners is far less important than curbing American demand through deflationary measures in terms of improving the nation's trade and current accounts. Indeed, the external strength of these economies in the mid-1980s is the fruit of sound fiscal/monetary regimes pursued by their governments, so that, in essence, the Japanese and West Germans have been following the path that America should have been pursuing all along. Perhaps there is room for more stimulative policies within these nations, but it is their officials who must remain the judge of that, especially since they have done a far better job of guiding their economies than their American counterparts on monetarist score cards. At bottom, the United States simply cannot afford to wait for changes to take place elsewhere when its own economy continues to be hamstrung by government deficit spending and headlong monetary expansion.

If there is anything the United States government can do to improve the country's trade performance beyond slashing its own outlays while keeping a tight rein on the growth of money, it is the elimination of impediments to the operation of free market forces within the domestic economy. In general, the monetarists welcome action taken of late to loosen antitrust restrictions,[90] to foster commercialization of innovations discovered through joint public/private research projects,[91] and to streamline, decrease, or expunge arbitrary export controls.[92] Taken incrementally, with a steady eye on transferring resources and discretionary latitude back to private enterprise, these measures conform to the monetarist credo of reducing government meddling in private sector activities. But, at the risk of redundancy, from the monetarist standpoint, the greatest hindrance to the American free market is the federal budget deficit itself, and unless prompt and decisive action is taken on this front, such ancillary reforms will go for naught.

CRITIQUE OF THE MONETARIST POSITION

The first objection raised by critics of the monetarist answer to the U.S. trade deficit is that its reliance upon substantial reductions in federal government deficit spending is not realistic in light of past, present, and prospective failures of Congress to undertake such cuts. Between the time of its enactment and the Supreme Court's ruling against it, Gramm-Rudman I did not lead to a decrease in America's 1986 budget deficit from its level of the preceding year. In March 1986, some $12 billion in automatic spending cuts were applied under Gramm-Rudman provisions, but, with essential services like federal courts forced to shut down, most of these cutbacks were countermanded by emergency appropriations, leaving the budget shortfall for fiscal year 1986 at about $220 billion, some $8 billion greater than in 1985.[93] The original Gramm-Rudman Amendment imposed a deficit spending

ceiling of $144 billion on the 1987 budget, but in the summer of
1986 both the Senate and the House of Representatives know-
ingly passed budget resolutions that exceeded this limit. The
Congressional Budget Office now projects a federal budget
shortage of $173 billion for 1987, $30 billion above the maximum
called for in the Gramm-Rudman plan,[94] leading Federal Reserve Chairman Paul Volcker to openly doubt whether fiscal year
1987's fiscal performance can even approximate that required
under the budget-balancing amendment.[95]

Both technical and fundamental defects in Gramm-Rudman
impede its capacity to force government to adopt budget cuts
equal to the task that the monetarists assign to it in improving
the country's international accounts. To begin, Gramm-Rudman
does *not* require Congress to actually meet its deficit-reduction
target in any given year, but only to predict that the budget presented for presidential approval will meet the ceiling.[96] Historically, yearly budgets prepared by the federal legislature are ultimately augmented by supplementary funding bills for unforeseen
cost overruns/revenue shortfalls by some $20 billion to $30 billion. Moreover, Gramm-Rudman simply sets gross targets without specifying how these goals are to be met. The significance
of this fault was apparent in Congress's hastily constructed deficit reduction package for fiscal year 1987. Facing certain presidential veto should it include any form of tax increase, this com-
promise measure projected a deficit decrease of $13.3 billion for
1987 without major cuts in military spending or domestic welfare
programs. How was this accomplished? According to its co-
sponsor, Senator Peter Domenici, the plan was loaded with "golden
gimmicks," including one-time savings, bookkeeping ploys, projected revenue increases through enhanced tax enforcement, and
sales of federally owned properties.[97] What we find, then, is that
in its 1987 plan, Congress merely forecast that it could reach
about one-third of the deficit reduction figure called for by Gramm-
Rudman by turning to makeshift cost-saving/revenue-boosting
devices, and thus avoiding the pain of even beginning to make
authentic spending cuts.

More basically, because President Reagan adamantly opposes
any new tax levies or increases to achieve balanced-budget program objectives, slashing expenditures is the only means of

reaching these goals. At the same time, since interest payments on outstanding federal debt must be made, the president rejects any large-scale trimmings of military outlays, and Congress is loathe to initiate decreases in Social Security payments/benefits, balancing the budget by 1991 through cuts in "unprotected" areas is just not feasible. As Richard Cooper informs us, meeting the 1991 goal without tax increases and without touching defense or Social Security would mean that "eighty percent of the remainder—law enforcement, foreign affairs, highways and airports and parts, welfare and health programs [other than Medicare], space, energy, agriculture and so on—would have to go."[98] Consequently, if the promise of Gramm-Rudman is to be fulfilled, either taxes must be raised or sacrifices must be made in politically sensitive areas, or the rest of the federal government must literally close.

The dismal prospects for adequate progress on federal budget deficits cast a pall over the entire monetarist approach for remedying America's external imbalances. At the risk of doing a disservice to the integrity of the monetarist prescription, let us assume that the dollar can be devalued (as it has been) against other major trading currencies without significant movement toward a balanced federal budget. As a general instrument for restoring price competitiveness to domestically produced goods in global markets, currency depreciation has proven to have only a temporary beneficial effect. In his empirical study of the impact of devaluation upon the trade and current accounts of nations undertaking, allowing, or experiencing it since World War II, Marc Miles asserts that currency depreciation was indeed associated with a minor improvement in the merchandise trade balance of those countries in the year following realignment, "but [the] improvement [was] small compared to the deterioration of the trade balance in the year of devaluation or in succeeding years."[99] As to devaluation's influence on the current accounts of these economies, Miles found significant improvement (after a one-year time lag), but this favorable trend was also temporary, lasting about two years on average.[100]

In this context, two interrelated points concerning devaluation are relevant. First, exchange rate depreciation normally generates upward pressures on domestic prices as the cost of imported goods, services, and production inputs can be expected to climb.[101] In 1971 and 1973, comparatively mild depreciations of the dollar contributed substantially to double-digit inflation within the American economy during the ensuing decade, and America's current trade imbalance is at least twice as large as those of the early 1970s.[102] Hence, one of the drawbacks of currency depreciation as a tool for dealing with the present trade deficit is that it is likely to result in a semipermanent increase in America's inflation rate. Moreover, as their real purchasing power declines through inflation, American producers and, most importantly, wage earners, will demand profit and salary increases to compensate them for inflation-induced erosion in their earnings. With the initial inflationary momentum thus reinforced, dollar-denominated prices will rise, wiping out the price competitiveness gains of the original depreciation for home-made goods in both domestic and foreign markets.[103] Coming full circle, the United States will be left with the need for further currency depreciation as a devaluation-inflation spiral is set in semiperpetual motion. Concurrently, devaluation makes American goods more appealing in world markets (in the near term), but it also enables foreign investors to purchase corporations and real estate, and other invertors to purchase corporations, real estate, and other physical assets at bargain basement prices.[104] In the abstract, after some brief relief for our external accounts, currency depreciation will leave the United States in the same circumstances as before the dollar's decline, saddled with higher rates of corrosive domestic price inflation and owning a smaller share of its productive capacity.

Acknowledging that part of the trade benefit from devaluation will eventually be canceled out through domestic inflation, monetary authorities, and, more importantly, foreign exchange traders often overshoot the mark, bringing the currency in question below the level warranted by macroeconomic conditions. Apprehensive about excessive dependence on dollar depreciation as a remedy for the U.S. trade deficit, Paul Volcker has warned: " 'History demonstrates all too clearly that a kind of self-reinforcing, cascading depreciation of a nation's currency, undermining confidence and carrying values below equilibrium levels, is not in the nation's interest or that of its trading partners.' "[105]

When a freely floating currency such as the dollar falls rapidly, holders of that currency begin to lose confidence in its stability and the soundness of the economy supporting it. If this occurs, the hard landing scenario outlined in Chapter 3 unfolds, the economy is plunged into deep recession, foreign exporters watch their sales in that economy's market shrink and potential foreign purchasers of the nation's goods are deprived of trade earnings to increase their import purchases.

Aside from the general deficiencies of reliance upon currency realignments to right America's trade balance, there are a number of questions surrounding the use of dollar depreciation to bring some of our present bilateral trade deficits under control. These questions revolve around two sets of phenomena, the first having to do with our trade imbalance vis-à-vis Japan, the second involving our deficits with important trading partners having currencies resistant to dollar depreciation. In their analysis of the potential impact of the dollar's decline against the Japanese yen, the research team of Stephen Haynes, Michael Hutchinson, and Raymond Miskell came to some disturbing conclusions. Tracing the movement of the two currencies over more than a decade and relating it to concurrent U.S.–Japan bilateral trade imbalances in manufactured goods, they discovered that American imports of Japanese manufactures are "essentially insensitive to exhange rate movements." [106] Even when the Japanese yen rose against the dollar, this did not reverse the trend of increased American purchases of Japanese wares. Because Japanese-manufactured exports to the United States are much greater in volume and value than American-manufactured exports to Japan, Haynes, Hutchinson, and Miskell deduced that "even a major depreciation of the dollar relative to the yen will not markedly reduce the present U.S. manufacturing trade deficit with Japan," and, more broadly, since one-half of America's overall manufacturing trade deficit is with the Japanese, "sustained dollar depreciation may not significantly reduce the U.S. multilateral trade deficit in manufacturing." [107] Studies of other bilateral trade relations confirm the low exchange rate sensitivity of American import patterns, so that in 1971–1974 and 1977–1980, periods when the dollar was relatively cheap against other G-10 currencies, real imports still increased at a brisk pace. [108]

Several factors account for the insensitivity of the U.S.–Japan trade deficit to exchange rate movements. The policies adopted by Japanese exporters are of the greatest significance in this regard. During times when their export earnings were favored by an undervalued yen, 1981–1982 for instance, Japanese manufacturers enjoyed yen-dominated profit margins nearly double those of the American firms they were competing against,[109] as voluntary export restraints (covering two-thirds of Japanese manufacturing exports to the United States in 1984), allowed Japanese producers to reap profit bonanzas. Consequently, even as exchange rates turn against them, Japanese export producers have already plowed some of these profits into product/process competitiveness upgradings and built up a "war chest" to resist the price impact of dollar depreciation upon their market shares in the United States. As Ezra Vogel observes, from 1971 on, every time the yen rose against the dollar, the American trade balance against Japan stabilized but did not improve because "Japanese firms simply restrained price increases to retain their shares of the [U.S.] market."[110] Most recently, in the twelve months from February 1985 to February 1986, as the yen appreciated some 40 to 50 percent against the dollar, Japanese producers increased their prices on goods offered to American consumers by an average of 10 percent or less.[111] According to a study commissioned by the Federal Reserve Board, if Japanese and other foreign producers chose to keep their profit margins thin during the dollar's descent they could preserve their American market shares intact for two years or longer.[112]

On the other hand, fixated with profit margins, American export- and import-competing businesses have historically chosen to lift their profits during periods of dollar depreciation rather than recapture/expand market shares at home or overseas. Compelled by currency realignments to hike their prices modestly in American markets, foreign manufacturers have had their fears of lost market shares assuaged as they watched U.S. corporations simply follow suit.[113] In like fashion, in her study of profit margins on American exports between 1977 and 1985, Catherine Mann reported that they did not fluctuate with currency movements. This suggested to her that American export producers departed from the practices of their foreign counterparts by failing to "nurse" external markets in hard times and "milk" them in good ones.[114]

One practice Japanese manufacturers have used to offset the deleterious impact of yen appreciation on their sales in the United States has been to shift part of their operations to economies that offer currencies which have not risen against the dollar. For example, in response to negative foreign exchange movements, the Japanese automaker Toyota expanded its production of cars in Taiwan and shipped the final products to the United States through the so-called back door.[115] This anecdote naturally leads us to the second major doubt concerning the wisdom of waiting for dollar depreciation to straighten out America's multilateral trade accounts. According to one set of figures, between the time of the Plaza Accord and July 1986, the yen appreciated some 51 percent against the dollar while the German mark rose by 33 percent.[116] Independent of significant progress on the federal budget deficit, in the monetarist understanding, this foreign exchange development bodes well for an improved American trade balance. Over the same span, however, the currencies of some twenty-five nations (accounting for one-half of American trade by volume) remained steady or declined against the dollar.[117] One year after the Plaza meeting, the Canadian dollar had fallen slightly against the American dollar, while both the Mexican peso and the Brazilian cruzado had depreciated substantially against it.

The governments of Taiwan, South Korea, and Hong Kong informally "peg" their currencies to the American dollar, so that the dollar's decline has produced a windfall for their exporters in third-country markets while enabling them to replace the Japanese in American markets.[118] Particularly in labor-intensive industries like textiles, where American producers face stiff competition from developing country exports, little relief has been forthcoming from the dollar's erosion against G-10 currencies.[119] In fact, much of the expected increase in American exports to Japan and West Germany from dollar depreciation has not been realized because exporters from countries like Brazil and South Korea have expanded their shares of these markets at the expense of both domestic and American producers.

THE STRUCTURALIST POSITION

Nowhere is the contrast between the monetarist and structuralist understanding of the American trade deficit more sharply etched than in the differences separating their respective remedies for it. While the monetarists insist that the trade imbalance must be dealt with through a reduction of the government's role in the economy, the structuralists contend that America's trade ills can only be cured through an expansion of public sector involvement. Specifically, the structuralists assert that the federal government must take the lead in developing an outward-looking industrial policy to reshape the domestic economy and enhance its ability to compete against foreign trade rivals.

Although the United States flirted with industrial policy during the New Deal era, the notion of government assuming an active part in restructuring private economic activity remained dormant after the modest experiments of the 1930s.[120] In isolated instances, as in some of the provisions of the Employment Act of 1946, the interventionist legacy of the New Deal resurfaced but in the early 1950s, the last institutional vestige of state capitalism fell by the wayside with the abolition of the Reconstruction Finance Corporation.[121] Experiencing a breakdown in the Keynesian approach to guiding economic development through macroeconomic policies in the late 1970s, the Carter administration made a short-lived effort to resurrect the concept of deep government involvement at the microeconomic level when it attempted to prop up the country's automobile and steel industries according to the suggestions of tripartite (business, labor, and government) committees.[122] The use of industrial policy as an alternative to broad macroeconomic management was stymied in the early 1980s as President Reagan's supply-side doctrines captured center stage. By the end of 1982, however, as the president's hybrid theories failed to yield satisfactory results and the American trade balance grew more lopsided, the term "industrial policy" was heard with greater frequency.[123] Often associated with the liberal wing of the Democratic Party, industrial policy enjoys backing from a fairly wide spectrum of political and ideological groups, and its support has broadened as America's external accounts have gone downhill.

The current campaign to implement industrial policy in the United States owes more to perceptions about what our chief trade competitors have done to strengthen their economies than to any model or precedent from America's past. As discussed in Chapter 2, the structuralists attribute much of the success of nations running large bilateral trade surpluses with the United States to their deft use of government-orchestrated industrial strategies for maximizing their national resources and America's corresponding lack of comprehensive planning.[124] It is by emulating the programs and institutional arrangements of trade surplus nations, particularly the example of Japan in following long-range plans that build up on its economy's competitive advantages,[125] that the structuralists see a means for reversing America's eroding trade performance. Hence, literally thousands of books and articles extolling the virtues of Japanese-style industrial management have been written as guides for the revitalization of American industry.

The task of detailing what its advocates mean in calling for the adoption of industrial policies to redress the American trade problem is severely complicated by the range of proposals advanced under this banner and the characteristic vagueness of individual programs within its fold. "Despite much discussion about industrial policy," Bela Gold remarks, "significantly disparate conceptions exist regarding what its basic objectives should be and what approach should be used to attain these objectives."[126] For some of its proponents, applying an industrial policy to the American economy does not require substantial alterations in basic organizational relationships, but simply heightened and more effective management of functions currently undertaken by government through existing channels. Industrial policies of this kind represent "little more than an essentially pragmatic set of suggestions to deal with some *ad hoc* problems."[127] For others, industrial policy denotes a revolution in how productive activity is organized and carried out.[128] In what follows, I will refer to the former as the *incremental* approach and to the latter as the *comprehensive* approach, and will devote considerably greater attention to industrial policy in its full-fledged, comprehensive mode. Although the incrementalists tend to be more specific in their recommendations for industrial change than their grandiose counterparts, they also leave a larger portion of these details for resolution through actual practice. Consequently, William Hudson's comment that "none of its advocates have formulated a detailed blueprint for how industrial policy should be carried out" [129] holds true for both groups within this camp.

Published in 1983, Ira Magaziner and Robert Reich's treatise *Minding America's Business* remains a standard exposition of industrial policy's basic features. In this text, the authors summarize the paramount aims of industrial policy as follows:

A rational industrial policy must accomplish two inter-related objectives. First, it must strive to integrate the full range of targeted government policies—procurement, research, and development, trade, antitrust, tax credits, and subsidies—into a coherent strategy for encouraging the development of internationally competitive business. Second, it must seek to facilitate the movement of capital and labor into businesses that permit higher value added per employee. [130]

In essence, a fully articulated industrial policy has tandem goals, and these dual objectives help to clarify the distinction between its incremental and comprehensive forms. Both modes acknowledge the need to make coherent and explicit that which government is already trying to do to enhance the international competitiveness of American enterprise. By intensifying these efforts, eliminating roadblocks to their workings and coordinating them with each other and with macroeconomic policy, the public sector can upgrade its record in assisting businesses to meet the challenge of foreign production. Regarding the second objective, that is, smoothing the movement of production factors out of declining sunset industries and into promising sunrise sectors, [131] the incrementalists either downplay or excise this function from their programs while those favoring an inclusive approach give it an equal or stronger priority in their ambitious designs.

Looking first at the instrumentalist model, most of these proposals for reforming how the federal government handles industrial policy functions center on expanding/modifying the Commerce Department or setting up new advisory/planning agencies. Bruce Scott, for example, would make the Commerce Department the focal point of industrial policy by broadening its powers and changing its designation to the Department of Industry, Trade and Commerce. Under his proposal, the International Trade Commission would be merged with Commerce, current export promotion programs would be expanded, and a formal mechanism for carrying on a dialogue between government and representatives of the private sector would be established.[132] Similarly, Senator William Roth has introduced legislation which would combine elements of the Commerce Department with the office of the U.S. Trade Representative to form a Department of International Trade and Industry including an Office of Competitiveness Analysis.[133] In the same vein, Penelope Hartland-Thunberg advocates the creation of a wholly new Department of Trade "that would gather together under one Cabinet-level Secretary the trade responsibilities scattered throughout government."[134] In modest contrast to these suggestions, Gail Schwartz proposes that Congress simply set up separate councils or commissions for specific industries to act as conduits for channeling feedback from the private sector to the legislature without rearranging the cabinet.[135] As to Congress itself, in September 1986, Senate Democrats put forth a "legislative blueprint" urging the formation of a sixteen-member National Council on Industrial Competitiveness staffed by delegates from business, labor, academia, and government. Funded at a level of approximately $500 million a year, the council would serve as a forum for identifying competitiveness problems and making recommendations for solving them, and would perform a handful of ancillary chores, such as monitoring technical advances abroad, promoting enhanced technical training in the nation's schools, operating a computerized national job bank, and so forth.[136]

All of these proposals limit the role of new or reorganized government bodies to one or more of three duties: (1) coordination of existing policies affecting the competitiveness of American business; (2) advocating new programs to improve private sector competitiveness; (3) seeking to harmonize ongoing macroeconomic planning, such as the budget process, with the country's trade/industrial interests. Amitai Etzioni stresses the first of these ends in suggesting that a National Economic Council "oversee and attempt to coordinate the diverse Federal programs that deal with the industrial affairs and to improve the efficiency with which they are delivered," [137] while William Dugger emphasizes the third of these roles in calling for a new planning body that would draw up long-range development scenarios as inputs for annual congressional budgets. [138] Despite minor variations among them, all of these incrementalist suggestions essentially restrict industrial policy to the first of the two objectives identified by Magaziner and Reich, with the second objective either dealt with indirectly or dismissed altogether.

The comprehensive approach to industrial policy is far more radical in its revision of government's role in the economy and hence much more controversial. Indeed, when its critics take aim at industrial policy they invariably reserve their sharpest barbs for this species of it. The key to comprehensive industrial policy is the endowment of government with novel powers to reallocate the nation's productive resources in accordance with changing global opportunities already at hand or looming ahead. [139] Rather than merely influencing the general course of national economic development through macroeconomic management, as Hudson points out, the comprehensive structuralist program hinges on the public sector's role in intervening "*selectively* to mold market forces." [140] Former presidential advisor Charles Schultze has captured the gist of comprehensive industrial policy, as distinct from the "blander" incrementalist version, in his statement:

What is new, however, is the proposal that government deliberately set out to plan and create an industrial sector, and a pattern of output and investment significantly different from what the market would have produced. Industrial policy thus aims to channel the flow of private investment toward some firms and industries—and necessarily, therefore, away from others. The government develops, at least in broad outline, an explicit conception of the direction in which industrial structure ought to be evolving and then adopts a set of tax, loan, trade, regulatory and other policies to lead economic activity along the desired path. [141]

Thus, in its comprehensive form, industrial policy broadens *and* deepens government involvement in the operation of market forces, directly contrary to the course espoused by the monetarists.

Organizationally, most inclusive types of industrial policy proposals rest upon the establishment of an independent National Board, similar in its autonomy to the Federal Reserve Board.[142] Alternatively called the National Reindustrialization Board, the Federal Industrial Coordination Board, the National Industrial Development Board, or, somewhat nostalgically, the Reconstruction Finance Corporation, this body would be manned by individuals from business, government, labor, and academia appointed by the president with the approval of Congress, and having either lifetime or long-term tenure. The board would be "empowered to collect information, convene hearings, coordinate international trade policies, intervene in certain Federal, state, and local regulatory proceedings, provide loans and guarantees for research and development, modernization or expansion and manage changing level of certain tax incentives and disincentives."[143] To handle this tall order, unlike incrementalist bodies, the board would have the authority to (1) make policy independent of other government agencies and (2) override the actions of other agencies which impinge upon its activities or interests. In addition, the board would supervise some type of National Development Bank as its funding arm. In most versions, the bank would receive an initial appropriation of perhaps $5 billion from either Congress or the Treasury Department and would be entitled to sell a much larger amount of federally guaranteed bonds in private credit markets.[144]

How would all of this work? A composite, but plausible, procedure would begin with the board surveying the national economy in an effort to distinguish "winners" from "losers." The former would be made up of those sunrise industries which appear to have a high growth potential and hold forth the promise of rapid productivity gains: in effect, those productive activities in which the United States has a current or prospective comparative advantage. The latter, of course, would consist of those sunset industries already declining under the weight of foreign competition, which lack the potential to increase their productivity levels: in essence, those sectors in which the United States has, or will have, a comparative disadvantage.

After it has separated the goats from the sheep, the board would convene industry-wide conferences with spokesmen from business and labor joining representatives of government and the scholarly community. This meeting would offer a further means for confirming, modifying, or reversing the industry's designation as a winner or loser, and would also permit both categories to participate in high-level bargaining sessions,[145] lending the process a pluralist or democratic dimension. On its end, the board would offer the industry in question a series of incentives to either expand or contract its productive capacity. For the winners the board would furnish subsidies, credit schemes, tax breaks, antitrust exemptions, and the like to accelerate their overall growth and encourage them to undertake high-risk, long-term projects on an individual and/or cooperative basis. For the losers the board would extend financial support, worker retraining programs, antitrust exemptions, etc., in return for reductions in capacity, divestiture from certain product lines, streamlining of management, etc., all aimed at creating a smaller but more competitive industry.[146] Having been given the opportunity to argue for or against the board's initial evaluation of their industry as internationally competitive or noncompetitive, and having hammered out a program for responding to this status, including specific commitments from individual firms defining their part in this response, each corporation would be free to participate in the final program (and become eligible for benefits through the board/bank) or to withdraw from it (and be disqualified from such benefits).

Many advocates of comprehensive industrial planning seem to imply that once an industry-wide restructuring scenario has been drawn up and individual participants have accepted their roles and learned their lines, the board's part would devolve down to the mechanical function of simply meting out undisbursed funds and other types of incentives, and the show would go on by itself. This inference does not stand to reason. The board would need to make sure that the individual actors in its cast were living up to their assigned parts; that, for example, a loser firm was actually reducing its production levels by a stated percentage. Having written the play, the board would be drawn into an ongoing critic/director role in administering a system of perfor-

mance criteria to monitor the private sector actors. In all likelihood, the board would come to resemble a domestic International Monetary Fund, supervising adjustment programs at the
microeconomic level. In other words, once the distinction between public and private sector functions has been blurred and
the customary threshold of government involvement in private
enterprise crossed, the board would be pushed toward continu-
ous intervention in the details of corporate planning and management. Thus, while its adherents insist that comprehensive industrial policy does not mean government dictation of basic
market activities, such as the setting of prices and wages, the
need to review the compliance of firms in meeting their restructuring commitments clearly unleashes a push toward deeper involvement.

CRITIQUE OF THE STRUCTURALIST POSITION

As one might anticipate, the nebulous vagueries enveloping
virtually all industrial policy proposals, especially comprehensive types, are an easy target for their opponents to hit. Paul
McCracken has characterized industrial policy as "a grin without a cat—an intimation that behind the brand name is a powerful, painless productive new approach to economic policy, the
details of which will be, but somehow never are, spelled out."[147]
In their ardor, zealous proponents of industrial policy appear to
present it as a panacea for what ails the American economy in
an age of intense global competition. But industrial policy is not
a costless cure-all. "Industrial policy in general is an essentially
meaningless concept," Gold tells us, because "it is inherently
impossible to improve and expand all sectors of industry simultaneously."[148] As we shall discover shortly, critics of industrial
policy suspect that its architects have failed to elaborate the finer
nuances of their proposals because to do so would expose some
glaring problems "better" left unspoken.

For many of its adversaries, the structuralist program for putting American industry on a globally competitive footing is la-
beled "industrial policy" in order to conceal its true stripe, that
is, a move in the direction of central economic planning common

to socialist systems. "Explicit industrial policies would pro-
foundly violate American ideological values and political traditions regarding the primacy of the market mechanism and limited government."[149] Seen in this light, industrial policy could
never be made acceptable in an exemplary capitalist/democratic
society. Moreover, the notion that government should lend a hand
to winner industries already on the road to prosperity will not
sit easy with an American public imbued with a deeply ingrained
tradition of fairness and equality (rather than efficiency) in the
distribution of the commonwealth's resources.[150] In contrast to
Japan and to West Germany, with their "heritage of shared responsibility and traditions of mutuality,"[151] the American ethos
is grounded in individual choice, not managed consensus, and
so, while industrial policy may thrive in these cultures, trans-
planting it to American soil is a different matter altogether.

In this same context, many American opponents of industrial
policy assert that its backers have either misread or misrated its
practice abroad. Citing the economic ascents of Japan, West
Germany, and Hong Kong, Bruce Bartlett contends: "The common thread running through all the economic success stories of
the postwar era is a heavy reliance on the private sector and a
government which cut taxes and allowed free markets to oper-
ate.[152] Scrutinizing a prime example of a foreign industrial policy
body in action, i.e., Japan's MITI, Charles Schultze points out
that in Japan's drive to global economic eminence, "the major
decisions about where funds would be invested were made by
Japanese business leaders, not MITI," Japan's laudable record
being a product of the "entrepreneurial vigor of private enterprise."[153] Noting that Japanese industry picks up 75 percent of
the nation's research and development tab and controls all of its
applications, one Japan-watcher has gone so far as to suggest
that the Japanese have fooled foreigners about the actual degree
of their government's involvement in private production, thereby
giving their trade rivals a bum steer in the direction of industrial
policy.[154] Added to this, according to the argument against
America's adoption of structuralist remedies, industrial policy
followers have generally overlooked numerous and important instances of its failures abroad. The British government, for example, spearheaded the development of its country's computer

and nuclear power industries, but neither has achieved substantial international success, while the joint efforts of the British and French governments to promote the Concorde passenger jet were not matched by a satisfactory commercial payback.[155] Indeed, in its opponents' critical litany, the most frequently mentioned examples of the shortcomings of foreign industrial policy are MITI's original conviction that the Japanese automotive industry would not become worldclass,[156] and its frustrated attempts to stop Japanese conglomerates from expanding automobile production for export.[157]

At one juncture, the industrial policy scenario has all interested parties from a particular industry sitting down at the same bargaining table to reach a common vision of the future development of that industry. From the start, this rosy tableau "ignores the political difficulty of reaching and maintaining agreement on values, goals, and objectives among diverse groups holding different values and representing competing interests."[158] Within any given industry, some firms will be larger and some will possess greater political clout than others. Hence, in theory, board/bank subsidies "should be allocated to those firms offering the highest prospective returns, "but in practice, the political process tends to allocate subsidies on bases other than pure economic criteria."[159]

The political obstacles to the economically rational working of the industrial policy process are greatly magnified when we expand the scope of critical analysis to the matter of just who are the winners and who are the losers, and, as importantly, which industries and sectors will be handicapped by failing to be designated as either and, hence, excluded from the industrial policy program as a whole. History is replete with instances of special interest groups coming to wield an inordinately strong influence over a particular government agency, as, for example, the commonality which often develops between an industry and a government regulatory body charged with overseeing it. Even worse, "the political power of old, declining sectors of the economy is usually greater than that of the new, developing sectors,"[160] so that established losers might simply overwhelm fledgling winners in exercising political pull over the board. And what of those sectors, industries, firms, labor unions, etc., not considered to be promising enough *or* depressed enough to qualify for board/bank support? For those in the middle, industrial policy will impose an indirect burden as government intentionally channels resources toward the extremes.[161] Indeed, for those export-oriented industries not favored by industrial policy treatment, a further disadvantage may arise from foreign governments retaliating against "unfair" American subsidization of select industries.[162] At both an economy-wide and an industry-wide level, industrial policy is vulnerable to political contamination, and no matter how strong the underlying criteria, the board's decision to deal with certain industries and neglect others is fraught with the potential for political intrusion and bias.

The selection of specific individuals to represent government, business, labor, and academia on the central industrial policy board creates both another problem and a broad paradox for the structuralist program in the minds of its opponents. If prominent persons from each of these fields are chosen to serve on the board, the public's confidence in its objectivity will be sorely compromised. In numerous public opinion polls big government, big business, and big labor have all been discredited to varying degrees, so it is likely that grassroots protests would arise to staff nominations and the decisions of the board.[163] As an alternative, the board could be filled with highly trained technocrats deemed to be experts in public administration, business management, labor relationships, etc.[164] While this would increase the acceptability of the board to the public at large, it would also act against the board's essential pluralism. In addition, unlike Japan or Western Europe, the United States does not have a strong and independent civil service tradition.[165] Consequently, if a technical elite is to run the board, finding suitable persons to staff it may pose a difficult task. There is, moreover, an overarching irony in the structuralist position here which has not escaped the notice of its more insightful critics. In the structuralist analysis, one of the chief causes of America's declining trade performance is the shortsighted and misguided policies of the government toward trade and industrial competitiveness. There is, then, an inherent self-contradiction in entrusting even broader decision-making power to the government to redress the trade problem, when the failures of the public sector have contributed so heavily to that very problem.[166]

This brings us to a final major rap which industrial policy's detractors have advanced against it. The entire industrial policy process rests upon the shaky assumption that the government has the analytical capacity to determine what the nation's industrial structure should be, who the winners and losers are, and how restructuring should be undertaken.[167] Commenting upon the failure of industrial policy to emerge within the E.E.C., Michael Hodges explains: "The problem here is that the Community's institutions . . . are no better equipped to make judgements about the winners of the future than are the member governments."[168] It is not simply that government lacks the requisite acumen to refashion the American economy, it is that no mortal body has the necessary set of economic criteria for deciding how the economy ought to evolve and how that evolution can be accomplished. "The limits of our understanding of the dynamics of the economy certainly do not permit us to adopt a fully articulated industrial policy."[169] Indeed, the lack of a reliable knowledge base for guiding industrial policy formulations is an even greater stumbling block when we consider that its field of analysis must encompass both domestic and world-wide phenomena. Should a comprehensive form of structuralist industrial policy be adopted, not only are individual mistakes likely to occur but, because of its integral nature, these errors will ripple through industrial policy plans as a whole.[170]

CONCLUSION

In search of a "quick fix" for the U.S. trade deficit, the federal government has followed the course of least resistance in the unilateral, multilateral, and bilateral dimensions of its trade policy. In each of these spheres, the operating assumption has been that the nation's declining ability to compete is the outcome of factors and policies beyond its borders and beyond its direct control. Such actions as do acknowledge an American part in the trade problem (currency depreciation, for example), have been pursued on a piecemeal basis, as if they were somehow unrelated to a basically healthy domestic economy. With political factors arising at every turn to distort them, the ad hoc, disjointed policies of the government substitute denials and knee-jerk reactions for the kind of systematic and methodical response the country's trade difficulties demand.

The U.S. government has shown neither the willingness nor the capacity to adjust its external accounts along monetarist lines. Both Congress and the president have failed to deal seriously with the federal budget deficit. The Federal Reserve Board has acted as an accomplice to continue fiscal profligacy, delaying the full impact of successive budget deficits through an imprudent expansion of the money supply. Since fiscal and monetary discipline are the essential elements of the monetarist approach for handling the trade imbalance, the tacit refusal of government to take this type of medicine makes it impossible for the nation to right its international accounts on a monetarist basis. Even if the government were to faithfully adhere to the monetarist prescription, the economy would necessarily undergo a contraction in its growth and increased domestic price instability. Finally, there are objections, both general and specific, concerning the efficiency of demand repression as the way out of America's trade woes.

The structuralists have been equally unsuccessful in convincing the government of the need for a comprehensive industrial policy to reshape American industry according to the requirements of a highly competitive global environment. In fact, apart from a handful of isolated reforms, their call for even an incremental approach to improving the public sector's trade/industrial policy functions has fallen upon deaf ears. The chances of the United States instituting a full-blown industrial policy featuring a central board/bank institutional mechanism are remote at best. Given the list of defects plaguing industrial policy in the abstract, especially its vulnerability to politicization and the absence of an empirically justified model for economic restructuring, the chances for such a program meeting the claims of its advocates are slimmer still.

NOTES

1. I. M. Destler, "Protecting Congress or Protecting Trade," *Foreign Policy*, no. 62 (Spring 1986), p. 100.
2. "President Reagan Issues New Trade Policy," *Business America*, vol. viii, no. 20 (September 30, 1985), p. 6.
3. Ann Cifelli Isgro, "Unwatched Trade Issues Come to a Boil," *Fortune*, vol. cxii, no. 2 (July 22, 1985), p. 105.
4. Scott Goddin, "U.S. Successfully Resolves Unfair Business Practice Cases Against Korea," *Business America*, vol. ix, no. 16 (August 4, 1986), p. 9.
5. Robert Z. Lawrence and Robert E. Litan, "Living with the Trade Deficit: Adjustment Strategies to Preserve Free Trade," *The Brookings Review*, vol. iv, no. 1 (Fall 1985), p. 5.
6. Steve Charnowitz, "Worker Adjustment: The Missing Ingredient in Trade Policy," *California Management Review*, vol. xxviii, no. 2, (Winter 1986), p. 156.
7. Robert Z. Lawrence et al., "Adjusting to Economic Change," *Economic Choices, 1984*, ed. Alice M. Rivlin (Washington: Brookings Institute, 1984), p. 137.
8. *New York Times*, August 6, 1986, p. D-2.
9. Destler, p. 96.
10. Ibid.
11. Ibid., p. 103.
12. *New York Times*, August 7, 1986, p. A-1.
13. *Economist*, January 18, 1986, p. 20.
14. Ronald Reagan, "President Reagan Reiterates Commitment to Free Trade Policy," *Business America*, vol. ix, no. 16 (August 4, 1986), p. 6–7.
15. *The Economist*, January 4, 1986, p. 35.
16. Goddin, p. 8.
17. Eileen Hill, "The Administration Is Working to Improve World-Wide Protection of One of Our Most Valuable Trade Assets; Intellectual Property," *Business America*, vol. ix, no. 15 (July 21, 1986), p. 9.
18. Edwin Meese and Malcolm Baldridge, "The Reagan Administration's 1986 Antitrust Proposals to Congress," *Antitrust Law and Economics Review*, vol. xvii, no. 4 (1985), p. 36.
19. *New York Times*, July 22, 1986, p. A-1.
20. *New York Times*, June 16, 1986, p. D-12.
21. Jeffrey H. Bergstrand, "United States–Japanese Trade Predic-

tions Using Selected Economic Models," *New England Economic Review* (May–June 1986), p. 28.

22. Destler, p. 104.

23. *Businessweek*, June 9, 1986, p. 31.

24. *Economist*, January 18, 1986, p. 20.

25. Reagan, p. 6.

26. *New York Times*, May 23, 1986, p. A-1.

27. Everett M. Ehrlich and Raymond C. Sheppach, *New Directions in Economic Policy: An Agenda for the 1980s* (New York: Praeger, 184), pp. 180–81.

28. James Greene, "The New Trading Stratagems," *Across the Board*, vol. xxi, no. 3 (March 1984), p. 29.

29. *New York Times*, September 22, 1986, p. D-7.

30. E. G. Jefferson, "Building a New Consensus on Trade," *Columbia Journal of World Business*, vol. xx, no. 4, p. 9.

31. Ehrlich and Sheppach, p. 182.

32. *New York Times*, September 13, 1986, p. 37.

33. Ehrlich and Sheppach, p. 183.

34. *Economist*, May 3, 1986, p. 79.

35. *New York Times*, September 7, 1986, sec. 1, p. 8.

36. *New York Times*, September 21, 1986, sec. 1, p. 1.

37. Robert Z. Lawrence, cited in *New York Times*, September 14, 1986, p. 40.

38. M. A. Akhtar, "Policy Options in the U.S.," *Harvard International Review*, vol. viii, no. 1 (November 1985), p. 14.

39. Destler, p. 105.

40. Bruce Levinson, "The High Cost of Keeping the Dollar Down," *Dun's Business Month*, vol. cxxvii, no. 2 (February 1986), p. 25.

41. Aloysius Ehrbar, "Toppling the Dollar Could Cost a Lot," *Fortune*, vol. cxii, no. 9 (October 27, 1985), p. 23.

42. Ibid., p. 20.

43. *Businessweek*, May 19, 1986, p. 43.

44. *New York Times*, August 15, 1986, p. A-27.

45. *New York Times*, August 21, 1986, p. D-4.

46. *New York Times*, September 22, 1986, p. D-1.

47. Daniel C. Brown, "Fighting the Tidal Rise of the Japanese Trade Deficit," *Business Marketing*, vol. lxx, no. 4 (April 1985), p. 79.

48. William B. Hart, *The United States and World Trade* (New York: Franklin Watts, 1985), p. 23.

49. *Economist*, May 17, 1986, p. 73.

50. Bergstrand, p. 27.

51. Susan J. Pharr, "Japan in 1985: The Nakasone Era Peaks," *Asian Survey*, vol. xxvi, no. 1 (January 1986), p. 59.

52. *New York Times*, August 1, 1986, p. A-1.

53. *Businessweek*, August 18, 1986, p. 63.

54. *New York Times*, September 9, 1986, p. D-1.

55. *Economist*, June 14, 1986, pp. 68–69.

56. Craig C. Carter, "Canada's Gambit," *Fortune*, vol. xcii, no. 11 (November 11, 1985), p. 126.

57. Rod McQueen, "Canada Warms Up to U.S. Business," *Fortune*, vol. cxi, no. 5 (March 4, 1985), p. 120.

58. Edwin A. Finn and Richard C. Morris, "Good Neighbors Again," *Forbes*, vol. cxxvii, no. 11 (May 19, 1986), p. 120.

59. *Economist*, January 18, 1986, p. 20.

60. *New York Times*, April 21, 1986, p. D-1.

61. *New York Times*, June 13, 1986, p. D-4.

62. Roy Howard Ginsberg, "The European Community and the United States of America," *Institutions and Policies of the European Community*, ed. Juliet Lodge (New York: St. Martin's Press, 1983), p. 173.

63. Ibid., p. 168.

64. *Economist*, April 12, 1986, pp. 33–34.

65. *New York Times*, July 3, 1986, p. D-1.

66. *New York Times*, September 8, 1986, p. D-1.

67. Bruce Stokes, "Korea: Relations Worsen," *National Journal*, vol. xviii, no. 18 (April 5, 1986), pp. 815–19.

68. *New York Times*, August 5, 1986, p. D-1.

69. *New York Times*, September 11, 1986, p. D-3.

70. Herbert G. Grubel, *International Economics* (Homewood, Ill.: Richard D. Irwin, 1977), p. 381.

71. Johnson, p. 297.

72. Martin, p. 699.

73. Marc Levinson, "Top Executives: Get Tough on Trade!" *Dun's Business Month*, vol. cxxvi, no. 4 (October 1985), p. 85.

74. Johnson, p. 297.

75. Cooper, p. 199.

76. *New York Times*, July 31, 1986, p. A-3.

77. McCulloch, p. 151.

78. Destler, p. 106.

79. Levinson, p. 24.

80. *U.S. News & World Report*, August 11, 1986, p. 41.

81. *New York Times*, August 9, 1986, p. 31.

82. *New York Times*, August 21, 1986, p. D-4.

83. Martin, p. 700.

84. *New York Times*, July 3, 1986, p. D-7.

85. Paula Stern, "The U.S. Trade System and the National Interest," *Vital Speeches*, vol. lii, no. 13 (April 15, 1986), p. 390.

86. *New York Times*, July 31, p. D-7.

87. *New York Times*, July 30, p. D-1.

88. *New York Times*, September 20, 1986, p. 33.

89. *New York Times*, August 9, 1986, p. 31.

90. David A. Heenan, "Building Industrial Cooperation Through Japanese Strategies," *Business Horizons*, vol. xxviii, no. 6 (November–December 1985), p. 13.

91. E. Jonathan Soderstrom and Bruce M. Winchell, "Patent Policy Changes Stimulating Commercial Application of Federal R & D," *Research Management*, vol. xxix, no. 3 (May–June 1986), p. 35.

92. *New York Times*, June 18, 1986, p. D-1.

93. *New York Times*, July 16, 1986, p. A-1.

94. *New York Times*, August 5, 1986, p. A-1.

95. *New York Times*, July 30, 1986, p. D-13.

96. *New York Times*, September 10, 1986, p. A-34.

97. *New York Times*, September 20, 1986, p. 1.

98. Cooper, p. 206.

99. Marc A. Miles, *Devaluation, the Trade Balance and the Balance of Payments* (New York: Marcel Dekker, 1978), pp. 117–18.

100. Ibid.

101. Jack Carlson and Hugh Graham, "The Economic Importance of Exports to the United States," *The Export Performance of the United States: Political, Strategic and Economic Implications*, ed. Jennifer J. White (New York: Praeger, 1981), pp. 129–30.

102. C. Fred Bergstein, "The Trade Deficit Could Be Ruinous," *Fortune*, vol. cxii, no. 3 (August 5, 1985), p. 106.

103. Paul A. Volcker, "Facing Up to the Twin Deficits," *Challenge*, vol. xxvii, no. 1 (March–April 1984), p. 8.

104. Ehbar, "Toppling the Dollar . . . ," p. 20.

105. *New York Times*, July 24, 1986, p. D-14.

106. Stephen E. Haynes, Michael M. Hutchinson, and Raymond F. Miskell, "U.S.–Japanese Bilateral Trade and the Yen-Dollar Exchange Rate: An Empirical Analysis," *Southern Economic Journal*, vol. lii, no. 4 (April 1986), p. 923.

107. Ibid., p. 931.

108. *New York Times*, September 21, 1986, p. F-2.

109. Edwin A. Finn, "Screeching to a Halt," *Forbes*, vol. cxxxviii, no. 2 (July 28, 1986), p. 39.

110. Ezra F. Vogel, "Pax Nipponica?" *Foreign Affairs*, vol. lxiv, no. 4 (Spring 1986), p. 763.

111. Aloysius Ehrbar, "The Super Yen Won't Save the Day," *Fortune*, vol. cxii, no. 3 (February 3, 1986), p. 66.

112. Finn, p. 39.

113. Ibid.

114. Catherine Mann cited in *The Economist*, June 28, 1986, p. 74.

115. Edwin A. Finn, "Good Medicine, Too Few Patients," *Forbes*, vol. cxxxvii, no. 7 (April 7, 1986), p. 31.

116. *Businessweek*, July 28, 1986, p. 24.

117. *New York Times*, September 19, 1986, p. D-5.

118. Andrew Tanzer, "The Trouble with Mercantilism," *Forbes*, vol. cxxxviii, no. 3 (August 11, 1986), p. 40.

119. *U.S. News & World Report*, August 11, 1986, p. 40.

120. Gail Garfield Schwartz, "The Hard Realities of Industrial Policy," *American Economic Policy: Problems and Prospects*, ed. Gar Alperovitz and Roger Skurski (Notre Dame, Ind.: University of Notre Dame, 1984), p. 79.

121. James K. Galbraith, "The Debate About Industrial Policy," *American Economic Policy: Problems and Prospects*, ed. Gar Alperovitz and Roger Skurski (Notre Dame, Ind.: University of Notre Dame, 1984), p. 93.

122. Amitai Etzioni, *An Immodest Agenda: Rebuilding America Before the Twenty-First Century* (New York: McGraw-Hill, 1983), p. 312.

123. William E. Hudson, "The Feasibility of a Comprehensive U.S. Industrial Policy," *Political Science Quarterly*, vol. c, no. 3 (Fall 1985), pp. 461–62.

124. Herbert E. Striner, *Regaining the Lead: Policies for Economic Growth* (New York: Praeger, 1984), p. 181.

125. Milton Hochmuth, "Analysis and Summary," *Revitalizing American Industry: Lessons from Our Competitors*, ed. Milton Hochmuth and William Davidson (Cambridge, Mass.: Ballinger Press, 1985), p. 391.

126. Bela Gold, "Some International Differences in Approaches to Industrial Policy," *Contemporary Political Issues*, vol. iv, no. 1 (January 1986), p. 13.

127. Paul W. McCracken, "Industrial Policy—The Grin Without a Cat," *Across the Board*, vol. xxi, no. 1 (January 1984), p. 24.

128. Ibid., p. 26.

129. Hudson, p. 466.

130. Ira C. Magaziner and Robert B. Reich, *Minding America's*

Business: The Decline and Rise of the American Economy (New York: Random House, 1983), p. 343.

131. George C. Lodge, *The American Disease* (New York: Alfred A. Knopf, 1984), p. 24.

132. Bruce R. Scott, "Can Industry Survive the Welfare State?" *Harvard Business Review*, vol. lx, no. 5 (September–October 1982), p. 83.

133. George Cabot Lodge and William C. Crom, "U.S. Competitiveness: The Policy Tangle," *Harvard Business Review*, vol. lxiii, no. 1 (January–February 1985), p. 42.

134. Penelope Hartland-Thunberg, "The Political and Strategic Importance of Exports," *The Export Performance of the United States: Political, Strategic and Economic Implications*, ed. Jennifer J. White (New York: Praeger, 1981), p. 33.

135. Schwartz, p. 87.

136. *New York Times*, September 11, 1986, p. D-3.

137. Everett M. Ehrlich and Raymond C. Sheppach, *New Directions in Economic Policy: An Agenda for the 1980s* (New York: Praeger, 1984), p. 106.

138. William M. Dugger, *An Alternative to Economic Retrenchment* (New York: Petrocelli Books, 1984), p. 191.

139. Gold, p. 21.

140. Hudson, p. 263.

141. Schultze, p. 4.

142. Lodge, p. 728.

143. Steven Schlossstein, *Trade War: Greed, Power and Industrial Policy on Opposite Sides of the Pacific* (New York: Congdon and Weed, 1984), p. 231.

144. Gar Alperovitz and Jeff Faux, *Rebuilding America* (New York: Pantheon Press, 1984), p. 267.

145. Hudson, p. 467.

146. Gold, p. 13.

147. McCracken, p. 27.

148. Gold, p. 18.

149. Glenn R. Fong, "The Potential for Industrial Policy: Lessons from the Very High Speed Integrated Circuit Program," *Journal of Policy Analysis and Management*, vol. v, no. 2 (Winter 1986), p. 265.

150. McCracken, p. 28.

151. Striner, p. 182.

152. Bruce R. Bartlett, *Reaganomics: Supply Side Economics in Action* (Westport, Conn.: Arlington House, 1981), p. 201.

153. Schultze, p. 6.

154. *The Economist*, April 20, 1986, p. 22.

155. Gold, p. 16.

156. McCracken, p. 28.

157. Schultze, p. 7.

158. Hudson, pp. 472–73.

159. Robert Z. Lawrence and Robert E. Litan, "Living with the Trade Deficit: Adjustment Strategies to Preserve Free Trade," *The Brookings Review*, vol. iv, no. 1 (Fall 1985), p. 5.

160. Murray L. Weidenbaum, "Japan Bashing and Foreign Trade," *Society*, vol. xxiii, no. 4 (May–June 1986), p. 45.

161. Fong, p. 265.

162. Ibid.

163. Alperovitz and Faux, p. 259.

164. Ibid.

165. Magaziner and Reich, p. 326.

166. Schultze, pp. 10–11.

167. Ibid., p. 4.

168. Michael Hodges, "Industrial Policy: Hard Times or Great Expectations," *Policy-Making in the European Community*, ed. Helen Wallace, William Wallace, and Carole Webb (Chichester, England: John Wiley, 1983), p. 288.

169. N. B. Hannay and Lowell W. Steele, "Technology and Trade: A Study of U.S. Competitiveness in Seven Industries," *Research Management*, vol. xxix, no. 1 (January–February 1986), p. 21.

170. Hudson, p. 474.

BIBLIOGRAPHY

Abegglen, James C. and Stalk, George. "The Japanese Corporation as Competitor," *California Management Review*. Vol. XXVIII, No. 3 (Spring 1986).

Abernathy, William J., Clark, Kim B., and Kantrow, Alan M. "The New Industrial Competition," *Survival Strategies for American Industry*. Ed. Alan M. Kantrow. New York: John Wiley, 1983.

Akhtar, M. A. "Policy Options in the U.S.," *Harvard International Review*. Vol. VIII, No. 1 (November 1985).

Alperovitz, Gar and Faux, Jeff. *Rebuilding America*. New York: Pantheon, 1984.

Amsden, Alice H. "De-Skilling, Skilled Commodities and the NICs' Emerging Competitive Advantage," *The American Economic Review*. Vol. LXXIII, No. 2 (May 1983).

Bailey, Victor B. and Bowden, Sara R. "Understanding United States Foreign Trade Data," *Business America*. Vol. VIII, No. 21 (October 14, 1985).

Baily, Martin Neil and Chakrabati, Alok K. "Innovation and U.S. Competitiveness," *The Brookings Review*. Vol. IV, No. 1 (Fall 1985).

————. "Innovation and Productivity in U.S. Industry," *Brookings Papers on Economic Activity*. No. 2 (1985).

Baldridge, Malcolm. "Secretary Baldridge Urges Japan to Lower Trade Barriers," *Business America*. Vol. IX, No. 16 (August 4, 1986).

Barry, John M. "U.S. Retreats from Free Trade," *Dun's Business Month*. Vol. CXXV, No. 4 (April 1985).

Bartlett, Bruce R. *Reaganomics: Supply Side Economics in Action.*
   Westport Conn.: Arlington House, 1981.
Beckner, Steven K. "The Boom That Won't Quit," *Nation's Business.*
   Vol. LXXIV, No. 4 (April 1986).
Belongia, Michael T. "Estimating Exchange Rate Effects on Exports:
   A Cautionary Note," *The Federal Reserve Bank of St. Louis
   Review.* Vol. LXVIII, No. 1 (January 1986).
Bergstein, C. Fred. "The U.S.–Japan Trade Imbroglio," *Challenge.*
   Vol. XXVIII, No. 3 (July–August 1985).
————. "The Trade Deficit Could Be Ruinous," *Fortune.* Vol. CXII,
   No. 3 (August 5, 1985).
Bergstrand, Jeffrey H. "United States–Japan Trade Predictions Using
   Selected Economic Models," *New England Economic Review*
   (May–June 1986).
Bernstein, Edward M. "The United States as an International
   Debtor Country," *The Brookings Review.* Vol. IV, No. 1 (Fall
   1985).
Birnbaum, Phyllis. "Honorable Fussy Customers," *Across the Board.*
   Vol. XXIII, No. 3 (March 1986).
Bowen, Harry L. "Changes in the International Distribution of Re-
   sources and Their Impact on U.S. Comparative Advantage,"
   Review of Economics and Statistics. Vol. LXV, No. 3 (August
   1983).
Brown, Daniel C. "Fighting the Tidal Rise of the Japanese Trade Defi-
   cit," *Business Marketing.* Vol. LXX, No. 4 (April 1985).
Caplan, Basil. "No Easy Solution to the Japan Trade Problem," *The
   Banker.* Vol. CXXV, No. 715 (September 1985).
Carlson, Jack and Graham, Hugh. "The Economic Importance of Ex-
   ports to the United States," *The Export Performance of the United
   States: Political, Strategic and Economic Implications.* Ed. Jen-
   nifer J. White. New York: Praeger, 1981.
Carter, Craig C. "Canada's Gambit," *Fortune.* Vol. CXII, No. 11 (No-
   vember 11, 1985).
Charnowitz, Steven. "Worker Adjustment: The Missing Ingredient in
   Trade Policy," *California Management Review.* Vol. XXVIII,
   No. 2 (Winter 1986).
Christelow, Dorothy. "Japan's Intangible Barriers to Trade in Manu-
   factures," *Federal Reserve Bank of New York Quarterly Review.*
   Vol. X, No. 4 (Winter 1985–86).
Cohen, Stephen S. and Zysman, John. "Can America Compete?"
   Challenge. Vol. XXIX, No. 2 (May–June 1986).

Cooper, Richard N. "Dealing with the Trade Deficit in a Floating Rate System," *Brookings Paper on Economic Activity*. No. 1 (1986).

Corbett, Mary Beth. "Commerce Department Analysts See Improved Year for U.S. Exports," *Business America*. Vol. IX, No. 7 (March 31, 1986).

Corrigan, Richard. "Industrial Policy?" *National Journal*. Vol. XVIII, No. 19 (May 10, 1986).

Cuddy, John D. A. "Some Reflections on Growth in OECD Economies," *Trade and Development*. No. 6 (1985).

Cummings, Bruce. "South Korea: Trouble Ahead," *Current History*. Vol. LXXXV, No. 510 (April 1986).

Destler, I. M. "Protecting Congress or Protecting Trade," *Foreign Policy*. No. 62 (Spring 1986).

Dreyfuss, Joel. "Japan's Sudden Slowdown," *Fortune*. Vol. CXIII, No. 7 (March 31, 1986).

Dugger, William M. *An Alternative to Economic Retrenchment*. New York: Petrocelli Books, 1984.

Eason, Henry. "Freer Trade Across Our Borders?" *Nation's Business*. Vol. LXXII, No. 7 (July 1984).

———. "Keeping the Trade Deficit in the Right Perspective," *Nation's Business*. Vol. LXXII, No. 10 (October 1984).

———. "Keeping Afloat in the Import Flood," *Nation's Business*. Vol. LXXIII, No. 9 (September 1985).

———. "Japan–U.S. Trade—a Dialogue," *Nation's Business*. Vol. LXXIV, No. 4 (April 1986).

Ehrbar, Aloysius. "Toppling the Dollar Could Cost a Lot," *Fortune*. Vol. CXII, No. 9.

———. "The Super Yen Won't Save the Day," *Fortune*. Vol. CXIII, No. 3 (February 3, 1986).

Ehrlich, Everett M. and Sheppach, Raymond C. *New Directions in Economic Policy: An Agenda in the 1980s*. New York: Praeger, 1984.

Enright, Joseph T. "Selling Consumer Goods in Japan," *Business America*. Vol. IX, No. 5 (March 3, 1986).

Etzioni, Amitai. *An Immodest Agenda: Rebuilding America Before the Twenty-First Century*. New York: McGraw-Hill, 1983.

Fairlamb, David. "Europe Struggles to Catch Up," *Dun's Business Month*. Vol. CXXV, No. 4 (April 1985).

Fiekle, Norman S. "Dollar Appreciation and U.S. Import Prices," *Federal Reserve Bank of Boston: New England Economic Review* (November–December 1985).

Finn, Edwin A. "Good Medicine, Too Few Patients," *Forbes*. Vol. CXXXVII, No. 7 (April 7, 1986).
———. "Screeching to a Halt," *Forbes*. Vol. CXXXVIII, No. 2 (July 28, 1986).
Finn, Edwin A. and Morris, Richard C. "Good Neighbors Again," *Forbes*. Vol. CXXXVII, No. 11 (May 19, 1986).
Fong, Glenn R. "The Potential for Industrial Policy: Lessons from the Very High Speed Integrated Circuit Program," *Journal of Policy Analysis and Management*. Vol. V, No. 2 (Winter 1986).
Fukushima, Kiyohiko. "Japan's Real Trade Policy," *Foreign Policy*. No. 59 (Summer 1985).
Fusfeld, Herbert J. and Haklisch, Carmela S. "Cooperative R & D for Competitors," *Harvard Business Review*. Vol. LXIII, No. 6 (November–December 1985).
Galbraith, James K. "The Debate About Industrial Policy," *American Economic Policy: Problems and Prospects*. Ed. Gar Alperovitz and Roger Skurski. Notre Dame, Ind.: University of Notre Dame, 1984.
Gall, Norman. "Hold the Champagne," *Forbes*. Vol. CXXXVII, No. 10 (May 5, 1986).
———. "A Yen to Spend," *Forbes*. Vol. CXXXVII, No. 11 (May 19, 1986).
Ginsberg, Roy Howard. "The European Community and the United States of America," *Institutions and Policies of the European Community*. Ed. Juliet Lodge. New York: St, Martin's Press, 1983.
Goddin, Scott. "U.S. Successfully Resolves Unfair Business Practice Cases Against Korea." *Business America*. Vol. IX, No. 16 (August 4, 1986).
Gold, Bela. "Some International Differences in Approaches to Industrial Policy," *Contemporary Policy Issues*. Vol. IV, No. 1 (January 1986).
Goldstein, Judith L. and Krasner, Stephen D. "Unfair Trade Practices: The Case for a Differential Response," *The American Economic Review*. Vol. LXXIV, No. 2 (May 1984).
Grant, Robert M. "Adjusting to a Strong Dollar: Lessons from the European Experience," *California Management Review*. Vol. XXVIII, No. 1 (Fall 1985).
Greene, James. "The New Trading Stratagems," *Across the Board*. Vol. XXI, No. 3 (March 1984).
Grubel, Herbert G. *International Economics*. Homewood, Ill.: Richard D. Irwin, 1977.

Hall, Harold H. "To Compete We Need Capital Accumulation," *Research Management*. Vol. XXIX No. 3 (May–June 1986).

Hannay, N. B. and Steele, Lowell W. "Technology and Trade: A Study of U.S. Competitiveness in Seven Industries," *Research Management*. Vol. XXIX, No. 1 (January–February 1986).

Harrigan, Anthony. "The American Economy and the National Interest," *Vital Speeches*. Vol. LII, No. 13 (April 15, 1986).

Hart, William B. *The United States and World Trade*. New York: Franklin Watts, 1985.

Hartland-Thunberg, Penelope. "The Political and Strategic Importance of Exports," *The Export Performance of the United States: Political, Strategic and Economic Implications*. Ed. Jennifer J. White. New York: Praeger, 1981.

Hattori, Ichiro. "Trade Conflicts: A Japanese View," *Vital Speeches*. Vol. LII, No. 7 (January 15, 1986).

Haynes, Stephen E., Hutchinson, Michael M., and Miskell, Raymond F. "U.S.–Japanese Bilateral Trade and the Yen-Dollar Exchange Rate: An Empirical Analysis," *Southern Economic Journal*. Vol. LII, No. 4 (April 1986).

Heenan, David A. "Building Industrial Cooperation Through Japanese Strategies," *Business Horizons*. Vol. XXVIII, No. 6 (November–December 1985).

Heinemann, H. Erich. "Why Not Have a Service Economy?" *Dun's Business Month*. Vol. CXXV, No. 4 (April 1985).

Hermander, Mark G. and Schwartz, Brad J. "An Empirical Test of the Impact of the Threat of U.S. Trade Policy: The Case of Anti-Dumping Duties,"*Southern Economic Journal*. Vol. LI, No. 1 (July 1984).

Hill, Eileen. "The Administration Is Working to Improve World-Wide Protection of One of Our Most Valuable Trade Assets: Intellectual Property," *Business America*. Vol. IX, No. 15, (July 21, 1986).

Hochmuth, Milton. "From Challenger to Challenged," *Revitalizing American Industry: Lessons from Our Competitors*. Ed. Milton Hochmuth and William Davidson. Cambridge, Mass.: Ballinger, 1985.

———. "Analysis and Summary," *Revitalizing American Industry: Lessons from Our Competitors*. Ed. Milton Hochmuth and William Davidson. Cambridge, Mass.: Ballinger, 1985.

Hodges, Michael. "Industrial Policy: Hard Times or Great Expectations," *Policy-Making in the European Community*. Ed. Helen Wallace, William Wallace, and Carole Webb. Chichester, England: John Wiley, 1983.

Hudson, William E. "The Feasibility of a Comprehensive U.S. Industrial Policy," *Political Science Quarterly.* Vol. C, No. 3 (Fall 1985).

Hutchinson, Michael H. and Throop, Adrian W. "U.S. Budget Deficit and the Real Value of the Dollar," *Federal Reserve Bank of San Francisco Economic Review.* No. 4 (Fall 1985).

Isgro, Ann Cifelli. "Unwatched Trade Issues Come to a Boil," *Fortune.* Vol. CXII, No. 2 (July 22, 1985).

Jefferson, E. G. "Building a New Consensus on Trade," *Columbia Journal of World Business.* Vol. XX, No. 4 (Winter 1985).

Johnson, Robert A. "U.S. International Transactions in 1985," *Federal Reserve Bulletin.* Vol. LXXII, No. 5 (May 1986).

Kahn, Herman and Pepper, Thomas. *The Japanese Challenge: The Success and Failure of Economic Success.* New York: Thomas Y. Crowell, 1979.

Kellner, Irwin L. "Crowding Out," *Bankers Monthly.* Vol. CII, No. 10 (October 15, 1985).

Kindel, Stephen. "The Falling Dollar," *Financial World.* Vol. CLV, No. 9 (April 29, 1986).

Kotabe, Masaaki. "Changing Roles of the Sogo Shoskas, the Manufacturing Firms and the MITI in the Context of the Japanese 'Trade or Die' Mentality," *Columbia Journal of World Business.* Vol. XIX, No. 3 (Fall 1984).

Krugman, Paul. "New Theories of Trade Among Industrial Countries," *The American Economic Review.* Vol. LXXIII, No. 2 (May 1983).

Kullberg, Duane R. "The Deficit Is Worse Than It Looks," *Fortune.* Vol. CXIII, No. 10 (May 12, 1986).

Lawrence, Robert Z. "The Myth of U.S. Deindustrialization," *Challenge.* Vol. XXVI, No. 5 (November–December 1983).

Lawrence, Robert Z. et al. "Adjusting to Economic Change," *Economic Choices, 1984.* Ed. Alice M. Rivlin. Washington: Brookings Institute, 1984.

Lawrence, Robert Z. and Litan, Robert E. "Living with the Trade Deficit: Adjustment Strategies to Preserve Free Trade," *The Brookings Review.* Vol. IV, No. 1 (Fall 1985).

Levinson, Bruce. "The High Cost of Keeping the Dollar Down," *Dun's Business Month.* Vol. CXXVII, No. 2 (February 1986).

Levinson, Marc. "Top Executives: Get Tough on Trade!" *Dun's Business Month.* Vol. CXXVI, No. 4 (October 1985).

———. "Comeback for Keynes?" *Dun's Business Month.* Vol. CXXVII, No. 1 (January 1986).

Lodge, George C. *The American Disease.* New York: Alfred A. Knopf, 1984.

Lodge, George Cabot and Crom, William C. "U.S. Competitiveness: The Policy Tangle," *Harvard Business Review*. Vol. LXIII, No. 1 (January–February 1985).

Magaziner, Ira C. and Reich, Robert B. *Minding America's Business: The Decline and Rise of the American Economy*. New York: Random House, 1983.

Marotta, George. "Our Domestic and International Deficits," *Vital Speeches*. Vol. LII, No. 8 (February 1, 1986).

Marshall, Robin R. "Japan and Germany: Recovery with Policy Stability," *The Banker*. Vol. CXXXV, No. 707 (January 1985).

Martin, Preston. "Statement . . . Before the Subcommittee on Economic Stabilization of the Committee on Banking, Finance and Urban Affairs, U.S. House of Representatives, July 18, 1985," *Federal Reserve Bulletin*. Vol. LXXI, No. 9 (September 1985).

McCracken, Paul W. "Industrial Policy—The Grin Without a Cat," *Across the Board*. Vol. XXI, No. 1 (July 1984).

McCulloch, Rachel. "Point of View: Trade Deficits, Industrial Competitiveness and the Japanese," *California Management Review*. Vol. XXVII, No. 2 (Winter 1985).

McCurry, Robert. "Competing with Japan: Will the U.S. Seize the Opportunity?" *Vital Speeches*. Vol. LII, No. 19 (July 15, 1986).

McQueen, Rod. "Canada Warms Up to U.S. Business," *Fortune*. Vol. CXI, No. 5 (March 4, 1985).

Meese, Edwin and Baldridge, Malcolm. "The Reagan Administration's 1986 Antitrust Proposals to Congress," *Antitrust Law and Economics Review*. Vol. XVII, No. 4 (1985).

Meltzer, Allan H. "How to Cut the Trade Deficit," *Fortune*. Vol. CXII, No. 12 (November 25, 1985).

Miles, Marc A. *Devaluation, the Trade Balance and the Balance of Payments*. New York: Marcel Dekker, 1978.

Minard, Lawrence. "Noah's Ark, Anyone? *Forbes*. Vol. CXXXVI, No. 4 (August 12, 1985).

Musto, Stefan. "The Loss of Hegemony: Sensitive Industries and Industrial Policies in the European Community," *Europe at the Crossroads: Agenda of Crisis*. Ed. Stefan A. Musto and Carl F. Pinkele. New York: Praeger, 1985.

Near, Janet P. and Olshansky, Richard W. "Japan's Success: Luck or Skill?" *Business Horizons*. Vol. XXVIII, No. 6 (November–December 1985).

Ohmae, Kenichi. *Triad Power: The Coming Shape of Global Competition*. New York: Free Press, 1985.

Pearce, Joan. "The Common Agricultural Policy: The Accumulation of

Special Interests," *Policy-Making in the European Community*. Ed. Helen Wallace, William Wallace, and Carole Webb. Chichester, England: John Wiley, 1983.

————. "Europrotectionism: The Challenge and the Cost," *The World Today*. Vol. XLI, No. 12 (December 1985).

Pharr, Susan J. "Japan in 1985: The Nakasone Era Peaks," *Asian Survey*. Vol. XXVI, No. 1 (January 1986).

"President Reagan Issues New Trade Policy," *Business America*. Vol. VIII, No. 20 (September 30, 1985).

Puth, Robert C. "Human Mobility as a Source of American Economic Growth," *The Quarterly Review of Economics and Business*. Vol. XXVI, No. 1 (Spring 1986).

Reagan, Ronald. "President Reagan Reiterates Commitment to Free Trade Policy," *Business America*. Vol. IX, No. 16 (August 4, 1986).

Reich, Robert B. *The Next American Frontier*. New York: New York Times Books, 1983.

Reich, Robert B. and Mankin, Eric D. "Joint Ventures with Japan Gave Away Our Future," *Harvard Business Review*. Vol. LXIV, No. 2 (March–April 1986).

Reinhart, Vincent. "Macroeconomic Influences on the U.S.-Japan Trade Imbalance," *Federal Reserve Bank of New York*. Vol. XI, No. 1 (Spring 1986).

Roosa, Robert V. "The Gap Between Trade Theory and Capital Flows," *Challenge*. Vol. XXVI, No. 1 (March–April 1983).

Ross, Ian M. "Successful R & D Management," *Vital Speeches*. Vol. LII, No. 12 (April 1, 1986).

Thibaut, de Saint Phalle. *Trade, Inflation and the Dollar*. New York: Oxford University Press, 1981.

Schlossstein, Steven. *Trade War: Greed, Power, and Industrial Policy on Opposite Sides of the Pacific*. New York: Congdon & Weed, 1984.

Schmenner, Roger W. "How Can Service Businesses Survive and Prosper?" *Sloan Management Review*. Vol. XXVII, No. 3 (Spring 1986).

Schultze, Charles L. "Industrial Policy: A Dissent," *Brookings Review*. Vol. II, No. 1 (Fall 1983).

Schwartz, Gail Garfield. "The Hard Realities of Industrial Policy," *American Economic Policy: Problems and Prospects*. Ed. Gar Alperovitz and Roger Skurski. Notre Dame, Ind.: University of Notre Dame, 1984.

Scott, Bruce R. "Can Industry Survive the Welfare State?" *Harvard Business Review*. Vol. LX, No. 5 (September–October 1982).

Skinner, Wickham. "The Productivity Paradox," *Harvard Business Review*. Vol. LXIV, No. 4 (July–August 1986).

Smith, Lee. "What the U.S. Can Sell Japan," *Fortune*. Vol. CXI, No. 10 (May 13, 1985).

———. "Japan Wants to Make Friends." *Fortune*. Vol. CXII, No. 5 (September 2, 1985).

Soderstrom, E. Jonathan and Winchell, Bruce M. "Patent Policy Changes Stimulating Commercial Application of Federal R & D," *Research Management*. Vol, XXIX, No. 3 (May–June 1986).

Stern, Paula. "The U.S. Trade System and the National Interest," *Vital Speeches*. Vol. LII, No. 13 (April 15, 1986).

Stokes, Bruce. "Intellectual Piracy Captures the Attention of the President and Congress," *National Journal*. Vol. XVIII, No. 8 (February 22, 1986).

———. "Korea: Relations Worsen," *National Journal*. Vol. XVIII, No. 18 (April 5, 1986).

Striner, Herbert E. *Regaining the Lead: Policies for Economic Growth.* New York: Praeger, 1984.

Takashi, Inoguchi. "Japan's Images and Options: Not a Challenger, but a Supporter," *The Journal of Japanese Studies*. Vol. XII, No. 1 (Winter 1986).

Tanzer, Andrew. "The Trouble with Mercantilism," *Forbes*. Vol. CXXXVIII, No. 3 (August 11, 1986).

Tanzi, Vito. "Fiscal Deficits and Interest Rates in the United States: An Empirical Analysis, 1960–84," *IMF Staff Papers*. Vol. XXXII, No. 4 (December 1985).

Tsurumi, Yoshi. "Japan's Challenge to the United States: Industrial Policies and Corporate Strategies," *Revitalizing American Industry: Lessons from Our Competitors*. Ed. Milton Hochmuth and William Davidson. Cambridge, Mass.: Ballinger, 1985.

Urata, Shujiro. "Factor Inputs and Japanese Manufacturing Trade Structure," *Review of Economics and Statistics*. Vol. LXV, No. 4 (November 1983).

"U.S. Trade Outlook," *Business America*. Vol. IX, No. 6 (March 17, 1986).

Vernon, Raymond. "The Analytical Challenge," *Revitalizing American Industry: Lessons from Our Competitors*. Ed. Milton Hochmuth and William Davidson. Cambridge, Mass.: Ballinger, 1985.

Vogel, Ezra. "Pax Nipponica?" *Foreign Affairs*. Vol. LXIV, No. 4 (Spring 1986).

———. "Dear America/Dear Japan," *Society*. Vol. LII, No. 4 (May–June 1986).

Vogt, Donna V. "Japanese Import Barriers to U.S. Agricultural Exports," *Congressional Research Service Review.* Vol. VII, No. 2 (February 1986).

Volcker, Paul A. "Facing Up to the Twin Deficits," *Challenge.* Vol. XXVII, No. 1 (March–April 1984).

Wallis, W. Allen. "Protecting Prosperity from Protectionism," *Department of State Bulletin.* Vol. LXXXVI, No. 2108 (March 1986).

Wang, N. T. "Penetrating New Markets," *Academy of Political Science of New York City Proceedings.* Vol. XXXVI, No. 1 (1986).

Weidenbaum, Murray L. "Freeing Trade," *Beyond the Status Quo: Policy Proposals for America.* Ed. David Boaz and Edward H. Crane. Washington: Cato Institute, 1985.

————. "Japan Bashing and Foreign Trade," *Society.* Vol. XXIII, No. 4 (May–June 1986).

————. "Learning to Compete: The Outlook for the 1990s," *Vital Speeches.* Vol. LII, No. 21 (August 15, 1986).

Whalen, Richard J. "Politics and the Export Mess," *The Export Performance of the United States: Political, Strategic and Economic Implications.* Ed. Jennifer J. White. New York: Praeger, 1981.

Wilson, Dick. "Japan: The Trade Challenge," *The Banker.* Vol. CXXXII, No. 675.

Van Wolferen Karel,. "The Japanese Economy," *Survey.* Vol. XXIX, No. 1 (Spring 1985).

Wolff, Edward N. "Industrial Competition, Interindustry Effects and the U.S. Productivity Slowdown," *The Review of Economics and Statistics.* Vol. LXVII, No. 2 (May 1985).

Woods, Clay. "The U.S. Computer Trade Surplus Erodes," *Business America.* Vol. VIII, No. 20 (September 30, 1985).

INDEX

About the Author

CHRIS C. CARVOUNIS, Associate Professor of Economics and Finance, College of Business Administration, St. John's University, is the author of *The Debt Dilemma of Developing Nations: Issues and Cases* and *The Foreign Debt/National Development Conflict; External Adjustment and Internal Disorder in the Developing Nations* (Quorum Books, 1984, 1986), as well as journal articles on related subjects.